THE

STORYBOARD

APPROACH

Advanced techniques for preparing
effective visual presentations

Marcel Dunand • Kerry Choun

ABOUT THE AUTHORS

Kerry Choun and Marcel Dunand are founding partners of BCD, a group of management consultants and trainers who specialise in coaching managers to communicate successfully within and outside their organisations.

BCD's clients are diverse in their businesses but have in common a need to communicate for results. Kerry Choun and Marcel Dunand also work closely with the IMD business school in its MBA and executive programmes.

The authors bring together more than 30 years of previous professional experience across such activities as graphic design, finance, management consulting, and consumer goods and industrial marketing. Their constant exposure to a wide range of businesses ensures that their advice and training is never academic, but practical and relevant.

ISBN 2-9700116-0-3

What is conceived well
is expressed clearly

Nicolas Boileau

FOREWORD

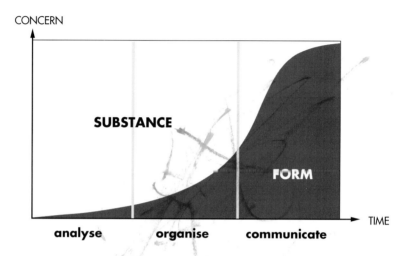

CONCERN

SUBSTANCE

FORM

TIME

analyse   organise   communicate

This book follows the three main phases of preparing a presentation as attention shifts from the *substance* to the *form*:

1. **Analyse**

    The presenter searches for the answers to a problem. This means extracting ideas from information and deciding how to express these ideas in the form of messages.

2. **Organise**

    The presenter then seeks to arrrange the different messages in a way that is clear, meaningful and convincing to the audience.

3. **Communicate**

    Finally, the presenter prepares the best medium and visual means to deliver the messages.

This books concentrates on the techniques of preparing and using the visual aids of a presentation - be it transparencies, slides and computer projections. These are collectively referred to in this book as visuals.

TABLE OF CONTENTS

Page

1 Extracting messages

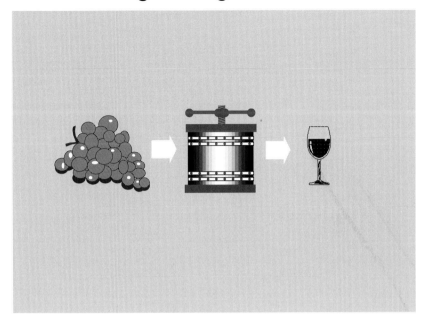

A message is the output of analysing information

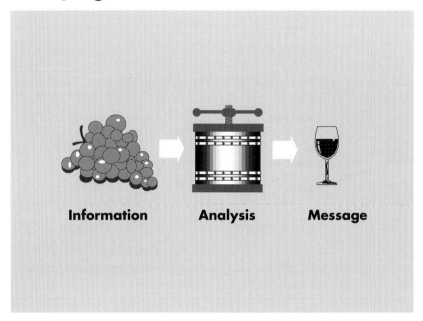

Information   **Analysis**   **Message**

Like grapes in the above illustration, information is only just raw material. Analysis is the process of adding value to information by extracting a message from it. Communication is about getting messages across to an audience. The impact on the audience depends on the quality of the message (wine) distilled from information and the medium (glass) for delivering it.

The process of extracting messages from information is fundamental to preparing what to say. If a message has not been extracted, then there is nothing to communicate...

Many conclusions can be drawn from raw information

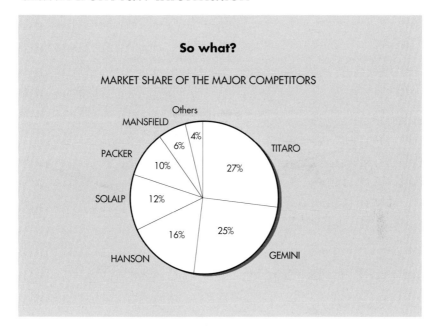

So what?

MARKET SHARE OF THE MAJOR COMPETITORS

People often confuse the subject (what you want to talk about) with the message (what you want the audience to know, to believe or to do). The chart above simply contains data from which several conclusions or messages can be drawn, e.g.:

· 6 main companies compete in this market
· The 2 leaders take more than half the market
· Titaro is the market leader

Each of these messages is an interpretation of the facts. It does not mean the manipulation of information. Each message is correct but one may be more significant and relevant to the presentation.

Drawing messages
requires taking a position

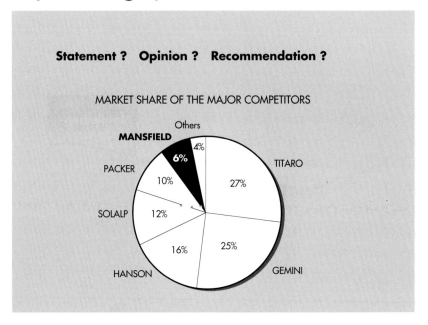

Statement ? Opinion ? Recommendation ?

MARKET SHARE OF THE MAJOR COMPETITORS

A message reflects one of three positions:

1. **A Statement** expresses facts. By making even a neutral statement, the presenter takes a position by highlighting what is important:

   e.g. Mansfield is 1/4th the size of the leader

2. **An Opinion** expresses a point of view. Factual messages on their own serve little purpose. Opinions interpret the significance of the available facts.

   e.g. Mansfield is too small to survive in this market

3. **A Recommendation** proposes the actions to be taken. It is usually supported by statements and opinions.

   e.g. Mansfield should merge with Hanson.

The messages in a presentation express the degree of involvement

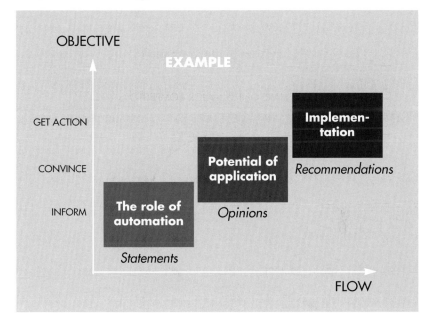

In seeking to obtain a decision, the presentation usually employs all three types of messages. In the above example:

- The first section describes the role of automation. The presenter lays out factual statements.

- The second section evaluates the potential of automation in the company. The presenter expresses his conviction and commits himself with opinions.

- The final section outlines an action plan. The messages are recommendations.

A presentation contains messages at every level

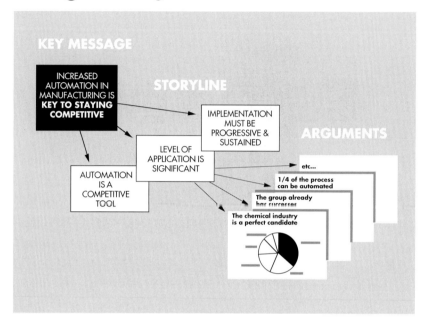

A presentation contains a hierarchy of messages.

Key message

In a succinct sentence, the key message expresses the global idea which the presentation tries to get across to the audience.

Storyline

It forms the structure of the presentation. Each section is summarised by a message.

Arguments

They are the individual messages of each visual. Each message is also supported by data or other details on the visual. Each message links logically to the next to ensure the flow of the presentation.

State your key message concisely as a sentence

"If you were to boil your book down to a few words,
what would be its message?"

Formulating a key message forces the presenter to synthesize the details to its most essential idea. This conceptual process can be quite difficult. However, once a key message has been found, it helps both the presenter and the audience:

· It becomes the focal point which directs the presentation.

· It sets a priority to select what is important.

· It gives the audience a ready-made sentence which they can easily retain and even pass on to others.

Each visual should contain a caption in the form of a message

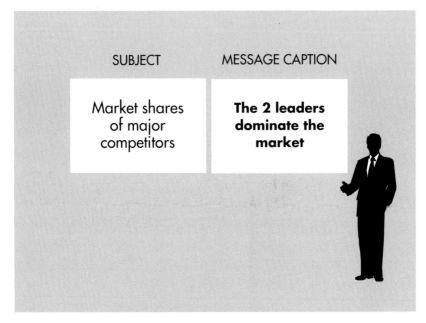

SUBJECT	MESSAGE CAPTION
Market shares of major competitors	**The 2 leaders dominate the market**

Consider the two captions presented above. They both refer to the same information. The left caption announces the *subject* of the analysis while the right caption is a *message* which presents a conclusion of this analysis.

Contrary to the adage, facts do not speak for themselves. The message has to be delivered. Displaying the message on the visual is a powerful technique:

- **It improves comprehension** because the audience can read the message and immediately understand the significance of the information presented.

- **It raises interest** by continually inviting the audience to react to an idea.

- **It saves time** by focusing the audience's attention on the essentials. The audience is less likely to be distracted by irrelevant or minor points.

A message must express a complete and value-added idea

"WEAK" MESSAGES:

"There are several reasons for this crisis"

"The rise in inflation is brought about by the following factors"

From the two examples above, the audience only learns that there are "several reasons" or "following factors" but nothing about their nature.

For the first example, a stronger message might have been:

"This crisis was caused by factors beyond our control".

A former U.S. cabinet member reportedly said: *"If we don't succeed, we run the risk of failure..."*

Choose the appropriate linguistic style for the message

A message can be expressed in different styles. The examples above refer to how foreign car makers are beginning to take a long-term view in building their businesses in Japan.

The **journalistic** style is meant to be catchy. However, the pun may be too subtle for some, and it is also difficult to link one such message to another. This style is appropriate for the title of a presentation to describe the overall theme.

A **telegraphic** message is a short phrase without a verb. It is easy to read but can also be ambiguous (e.g. do they or do they not have a long term view?). Being shorter, this style is suitable for summarising the sections of the presentation.

The **complete** sentence is longer but is clear and reads easily. Also, each message can be linked to the next. We recommend this style for the captions to the visuals.

Messages form the
substance of a presentation

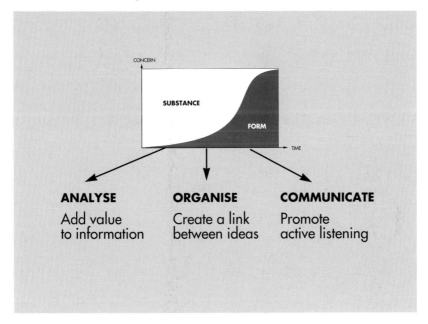

Messages are essential in all three phases of preparing a presentation.

Analyse

The purpose of analysis is to distil the essence from raw information.
Messages express what is essential. The process of extracting
messages forces the presenter to add value to information and to be
rigorous in his thinking by forcing him to consider what he really wants
to say.

Organise

From the raw collection of data, messages allow the presenter to create
a hierarchy and flow of ideas.

Communicate

Finally, clearly written messages capture the audience's interest, focus
their attention and invite them to react.

2 Grouping information

sunroof

airbags

heated seats

power windows

seat belts

roadholding

anti-locking brakes

consumption

air conditioner

lateral protection

anti-skid system

acceleration

performance

Grouping makes information meaningful...

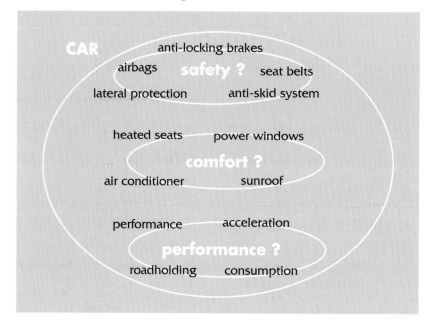

The average human mind is unable to cope with random or too much information at a time. In reading the list in the previous page, we intuitively induce that the items relate to a car and we try to group them. These items then begin to make sense.

...by giving a higher level of insight

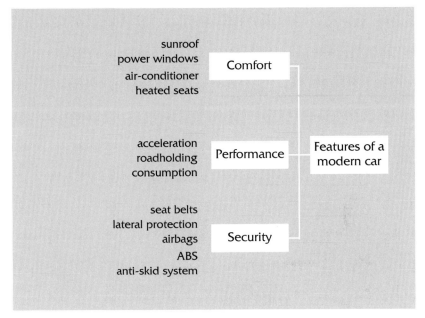

Grouping is powerful analytical technique. In the process of synthesis, grouping distils a higher level of insight from the details.

Grouping is also an equally powerful communication tool. Information which is grouped becomes more meaningful and memorable.

Grouping is a creative
process but must be logical

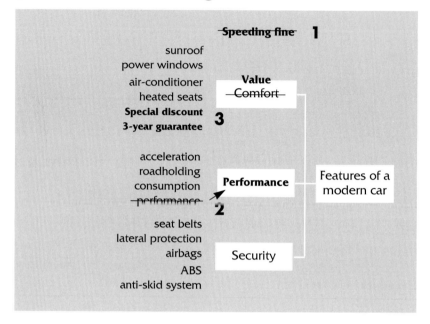

Grouping follows an inductive thinking process that conforms to rules of logic:

1. The items in a group must be of the same **type**

   e.g., we cannot fit a new item *speeding fine* into any of the existing groups.

2. The items in a group must be of the same hierarchical **level**

   e.g., although performance is one of the items, it actually groups three other items in the list.

3. The description of a group must cover **all** the described items

   e.g., if two new items *special discount* and *3-year guarantee*, are included, we can create a new group called *value* which includes the *comfort* features.

A big group can be further sub-classified

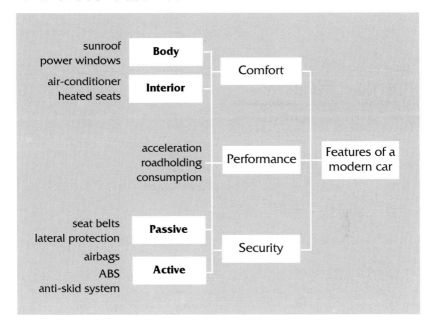

A long list of items belonging to a group can be sub-classified to make the information even more meaningful.

Grouping also applies to ideas

Running...

- tones the muscles
- increases energy level
- requires little equipment
- strengthens the heart
- raises morale
- is good at any age
- heightens concentration

Summarise each group
of ideas with a message

RUNNING BENEFITS EVERYONE

It improves your health...
- tones the muscles
- strengthens the heart
- improves breathing

...makes you work better
- increases energy level
- heightens concentration
- raises morale

...and is easy to do
- is good at any age
- requires little equipment
- can be practised anywhere

Grouping also applies to ideas. After putting similar ideas together, classify them with a message.

In the above example, the arguments in favour of running are grouped into the *physical, psychological* and *practical* advantages of running.

3 Assessing the Situation

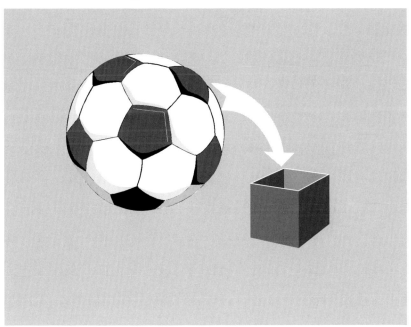

Adapt the presentation
to the situation

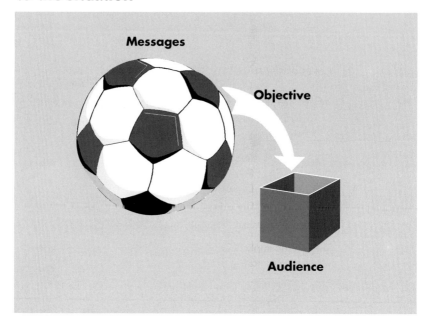

Assessing the situation is like working out how to fit the ball
(messages) into the box, It involves thinking about two inter-related
issues:

Objective

Presentations are not an end in themself. After the presentation, what
should the audience know, accept and do?

Audience

An audience is a customer. Making a presentation is like selling ideas
to them. What are their views on the subject? What are their choices?
What would make them respond favourably?

Clarify the OBJECTIVE -
what do you plan to achieve?

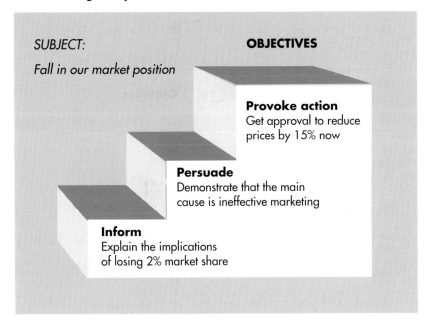

SUBJECT:

Fall in our market position

OBJECTIVES

Provoke action
Get approval to reduce
prices by 15% now

Persuade
Demonstrate that the main
cause is ineffective marketing

Inform
Explain the implications
of losing 2% market share

Surprisingly, many presenters do not think about what they want to achieve, other than talking about the subject (*e.g. the fall in market position*). Consequently, the presentation lacks a sense of purpose.

The presenter should know how far he needs to go:

- **To inform** is the basic reason for all communication. An informative presentation is factual and descriptive.

- **To convince** is to get the audience to share your point of view. Facts alone are not enough to persuade. An audience does not necessarily understand the issue or draw the same conclusions. The speaker has to express his opinions.

- **To provoke action** is the highest aim of communication. It often requires going through the first two steps but always ends with recommendations.

A presentation is more effective than a document in motivating an audience to act

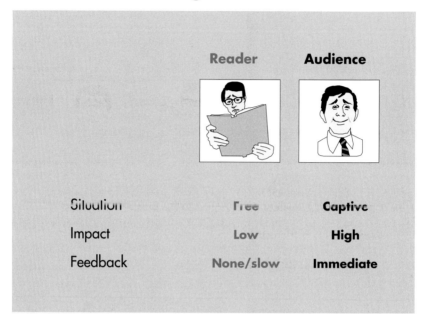

	Reader	Audience
Situation	Free	Captive
Impact	Low	High
Feedback	None/slow	Immediate

Choose to present rather than write if you want to communicate information urgently and if you want the audience to act. An audience is more active than a reader.

Situation

An audience is captive while the reader reads at leisure i.e. when he wants, where he wants, and *if* he wants...

Impact

The speaker gets his messages across directly. He also interacts with the audience and communicates through his tone, gestures and energy level.

Feedback

The audience gives continual feedback, directly or through the behaviour. The presenter is able to correct misunderstanding, and to detect and overcome objections. He can even ask for an immediate response. The reader does not feel obliged to respond.

However, an audience
is handicapped

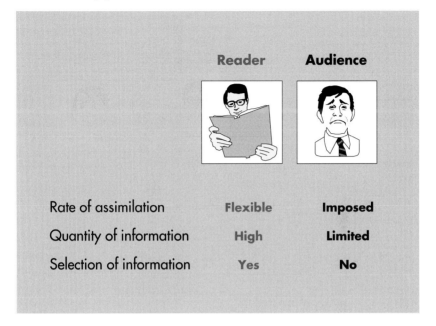

	Reader	Audience
Rate of assimilation	Flexible	Imposed
Quantity of information	High	Limited
Selection of information	Yes	No

Unlike the reader, an audience faces several obstacles:

Rate of assimilation

A reader decides his own pace. He can spend three minutes or an hour on a chart. The audience is constrained by the rhythm imposed by the presenter.

Quantity of information

A document can be as long as required since the reader can stop and start at will. On the other hand, an audience can only absorb so much information at a time.

Selection of information

The reader flips through a document and chooses to read only what interests him. The audience cannot listen selectively.

To be effective, a presentation must overcome the handicap of an audience

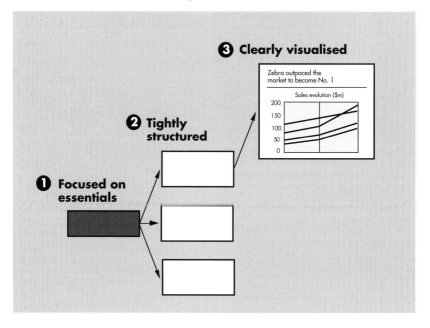

To do this, a presentation must meet at least three conditions:

Focused on essentials

Think of the presentation as the introduction to a debate. Present only what must be said. Keep as "backup" what is worth saying if you have the time, or use it in discussions to elaborate a detail.

Tightly structured

An audience should be able to understand the link between the different parts of a speech. Unlike a book, the audience cannot refer backward and forward to a speech.

Clearly visualised

Visual aids reinforce the message by making what is said easier to understand and remember. Visuals illustrate the basic information while oral comments complete it.

Knowing your AUDIENCE enables you to approach them correctly

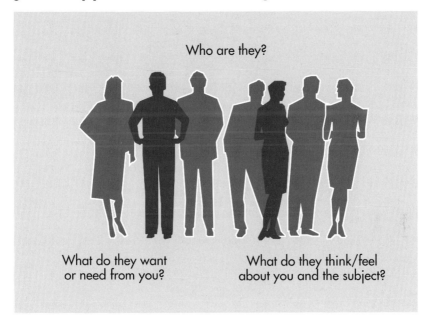

Who are they?

What do they want
or need from you?

What do they think/feel
about you and the subject?

Who are they?

The bigger the audience, the more difficult it is to meet the expectations of everyone. Concentrate on those who make the decisions or influence the others. Be aware that the most senior person is not always your target audience.

What do they want or need from you?

That depends on their position, background and level of knowledge or interest in the subject. Their expectations determine the language you should use, and the scope or depth of details you should cover.

What do they think/feel about you and the subject?

Put yourself in their shoes. What is their position on the subject? Do they have any pre-conceived objections? How will your conclusions affect their personal interests? Are you credible in their eyes? Their attitude influences the structure and tone of the presentation.

Each type of audience requires a different strategy

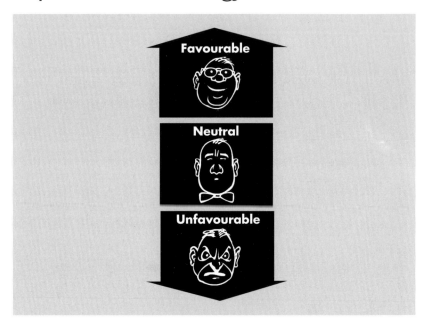

The presenter faces three general types of audience.

- **Favourable** audiences are on your side. They range from people who simply share your views to enthusiastic fans. If they already agree, what do we have to tell them?

- **Neutral** audiences do not have a position - they are neither for nor against you. They consist of people who are uninterested, undecided or uninformed.

- **Unfavourable** audiences are challenging. They range from people who disagree passively to those who are hostile.

The presenter must be realistic in expecting how much he can achieve with his audience. He is unlikely to turn a hostile audience into a friendly one. Knowing the audience permits the presenter to conceive an effective strategy.

With a favourable audience, concentrate on getting results

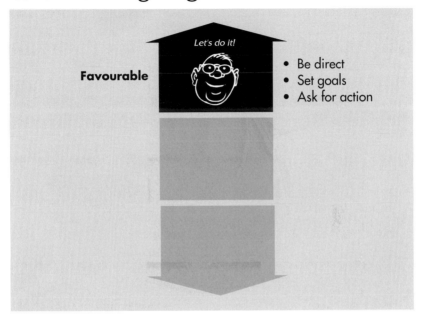

An audience may agree with you but they do not necessarily know what to do. The challenge with a favourable audience is to build on their enthusiasm. Move from "*Yes, I agree*" to "*Let's do it*". In general, with a supportive audience:

Be direct

Do not oversell by giving further proofs and arguments to an audience who is already convinced. Be direct and let them know from the start what your key messages are.

Set goals

Get commitments to action by agreeing on objectives. Remind them of what they stand to gain or lose.

Ask for action

Express clearly what needs or remains to be done, and what their roles are. Prompt them to quick action.

Move a
neutral audience

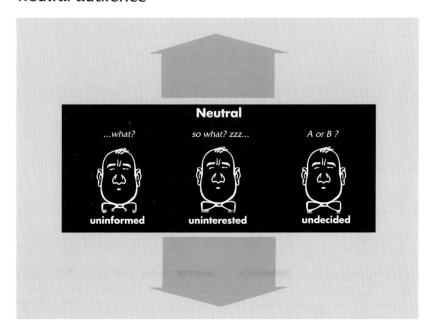

Neutral audiences are in a state of inaction.

Uninformed audiences must see the need to know. Put questions into their minds. Establish your credibility and present the subject with a clear structure. Do not overwhelm them with information - encourage them to ask and learn.

Uninterested audiences feel detached. Ask for their support by helping them to visualise the benefits (or risks). Give specific examples and avoid conceptual arguments. Get them involved by proposing something they can accept and do readily.

Undecided audiences are usually well-informed. Giving even more facts rarely tips the balance. Instead, focus on selected points and change the audience's perception or assessment of them. Illustrate with real examples. To help them decide, propose something easier to accept (*"What have you got to lose?"*).

With an unfavourable audience, build on areas of agreement

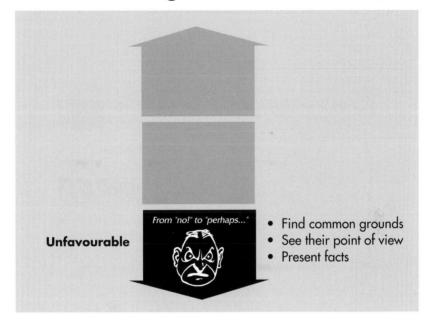

Unfavourable

From "no!" to "perhaps..."

- Find common grounds
- See their point of view
- Present facts

The over-riding objective is to make progress.

Find common grounds

Start with areas of agreement. Organise the presentation into independent sections so that a proposal is not rejected because of disagreement over one issue. Be realistic on what you can achieve at one time - aim to move them from "*I disagree...*" to "*perhaps...*"

See their point of view

Show that you understand their position. Describe their arguments in your words. This reduces the impact of *their* arguments when they bring them up later. Be clear about where you disagree.

Present facts and evidence

Show where your information comes from. Refer to experts and authorities. The negative audience is NOT interested in what *you* believe and why *you* are convinced.

Assessing the situation
helps you shape the approach

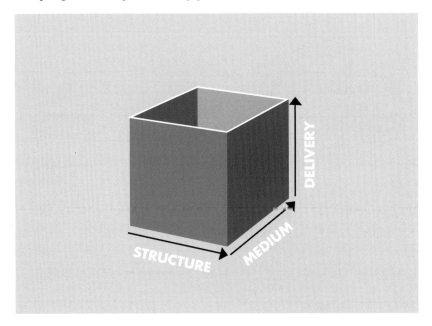

Assessing the situation is critical in planning and organising a presentation. The presenter shapes his approach in at least three ways:

Structure

The presenter decides whether to approach the subject *directly* or *indirectly* in his approach, and whether to build his arguments in *parallel* or in a *linked* step-by-step fashion (more about this later). He identifies what and how much information to include.

Medium

From the flip chart to transparencies to a animated multi-media show, the presenter has a variety of media to choose from. Each medium has its strengths and weaknesses. The presenter selects a medium to suit the situation.

Delivery

The speaker adapts his *tone* and *style* to the nature of the meeting, and his *language* to the profile of his audience.

Structuring the content

KEY MESSAGE

Summary

Supporting details

ELECTRONIC MONEY

So much for the cashless society

...rmation of the Internet from a huge virtual com...
virtual economy may herald the age of electron...
with it, headaches for traditional banks and regula...

Unless the Internet embraces commerce, it runs the risk of going the way of CB radio. If people aren't making money, they won't add value and this won't work". So thinks Lee Stein, a Californian lawyer, accountant and entrepreneur , who is a man with a vested interest. His First Virtual Holdings, billed ambitiously as the world's first truly electronic bank, opened its (virtual) doors on October 17th.

About 30m people and 20,000 firms around the world use the ...et, a term coined to describe ...ity of computers and ...tworks able to talk to ...a telecommunica- ...mon data

What they lack is the means to buy from their keyboard, on impulse. They could pay by credit card, transmitting the necessary data by modem; but intercepting messages on the Internet is trivially easy for a smart hacker, so sending a credit-card number in an unscrambled message is inviting trouble. It would be relatively safe to send a credit-card number encrypted with a hard-to break code; but that would require either a general encoding protocols (which might happen, but has not done so yet), or the making of prior ad hoc arrangements between buyers and sellers.

The Internet has b...

Source: The Economist

Do not communicate in the way you have analysed the subject

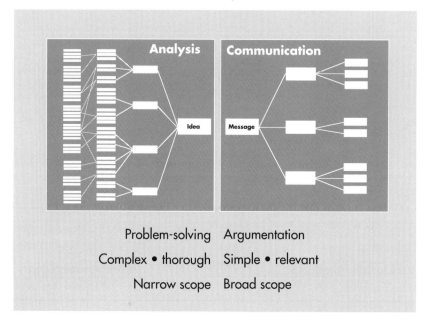

Analysis	**Communication**

Problem-solving   Argumentation

Complex • thorough   Simple • relevant

Narrow scope   Broad scope

Process

Analysis is directed to solving a problem while communication sells the answer. The process used to reach a conclusion is not always the best one to explain that conclusion.

Information

An analysis may be complex but communication must always be simple. Advocating a position does not mean showing all the results of your analysis but rather explaining its relevance to the issue.

Scope

Communication is about achieving results in organisations. It necessarily involves other people and must therefore take into account their concerns, assumptions and opinions.

A presentation is made up of a hierarchy of messages

Key message	Storyline	Arguments
	Further growth in both sales & profits...	• Sales up 20% • Profit up 21% • Margin strong - 10% • Prices competitive
Further strong growth rewards our shareholder	...from continued expansion in new stores & products...	• Existing stores improve • 15 new stores • New D.I.Y. lines
	...allows an interim dividend of $1.	• 20% increase • Paid 30 Jan • For shareholders on register on 21 Dec

A presentation is like an iceberg and the messages it contains fit into a hierarchy:

- Like the visible tip of an iceberg, a presentation must be focused with one *key* or *overall message*. The full detailed analysis remains submerged and unseen.
- The contents are organised into a storyline with three main sections.
- Each section is in turn supported by *arguments* or descriptions.

Keep the structure simple - limit it to three sections

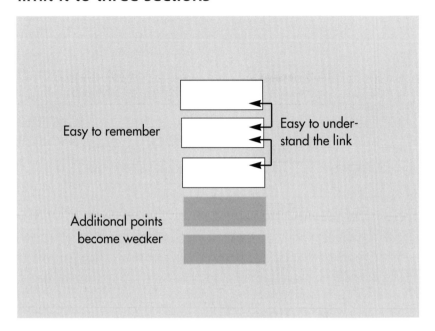

An simple structure is an effective one. Organise the entire contents of a presentation into three sections:

- **It is easy to remember**

  The typical audience has difficulty remembering more than three items.

- **It is easy to understand the link**

  It is easy to see how three parts relate to one another. A fourth element complicates the link.

- **Additional points become weaker**

  If the three strongest arguments are not enough to get your messages across or to persuade the audience, adding more arguments will not compensate for what is lacking. Moreover, the presenter exposes himself by giving the audience a better chance to attack the weak arguments!

The structure can be parallel or linked

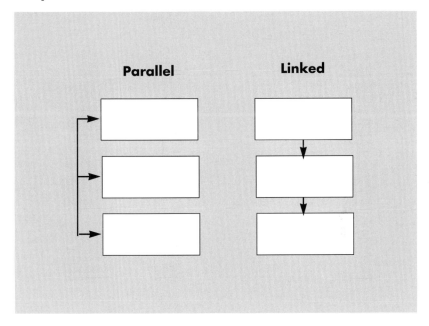

Parallel arguments

The parallel structure consists of three similar arguments (e.g. reasons) which complement each other. They are like the legs of a tripod and follow an inductive reasoning process.

Linked arguments

The linked structure is sequential. One argument builds on the previous argument and carries it further. They are like the steps of a ladder and follow a deductive reasoning process.

Parallel arguments are clear and direct

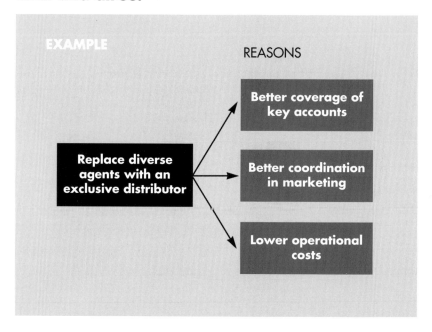

Parallel arguments are suitable for presenting a simple subject to a neutral or favourable audience. A key message is supported by a list of causes, effects, advantages, reasons, features, etc.

The order of the arguments can be changed. However, it is advisable to put the strongest argument either at the beginning or at the end.

A strong feature of the parallel structure is that the overall conclusion is not totally destroyed even if one of the supporting arguments is challenged.

Parallel arguments are popular in sales and advertising: e.g. *whiter, brighter and cleaner.*

Linked arguments lead the audience through logical or analytical steps

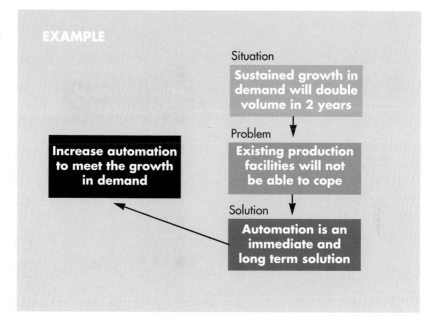

Situation

Sustained growth in demand will double volume in 2 years

Problem

Increase automation to meet the growth in demand

Existing production facilities will not be able to cope

Solution

Automation is an immediate and long term solution

Linked arguments are appropriate for a difficult subject or an unfavourable audience. We start from what is generally accepted or familiar, and lead step by step to the final conclusion.

Linked arguments are powerful. As arguments are built logically, an audience cannot easily "back-track" and reject a new idea which is built on a point accepted earlier.

On the other hand, if the audience successfully challenges any of the steps, the subsequent conclusion is no longer valid. In the above example, if an audience is able to demonstrate that demand will not double but only increase by 30%, then the link in the argument collapses.

Linked arguments overcome one obstacle at a time

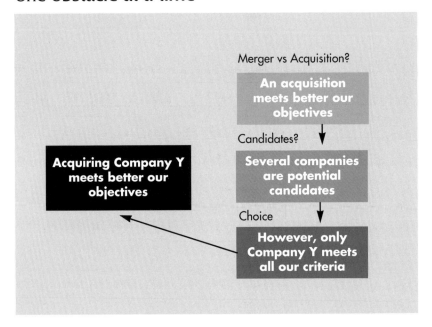

Linked arguments are particularly appropriate in situations where the audience has preconceived ideas which are opposite or different to what you are about to present.

In the above example, suppose a work group is assigned to study the feasibility of merging with Company X.   They then concluded that it would in fact be better to *acquire* Company *Y.*

There are two issues: *merging vs acquiring* and *Company X vs Y.* Linked arguments overcome one issue at a time.

Choose a structure which reflects how the audience thinks about the subject

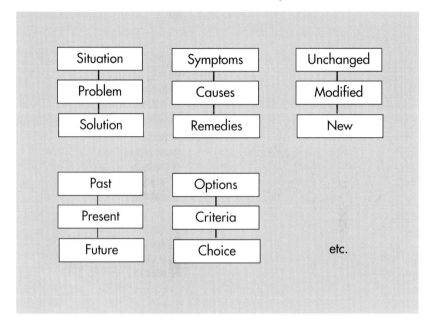

The best structure is one that is familiar and relevant to the audience. Here are other examples of linked arguments:

- Two-sided or "strawman" approach

Point	*Machine A is the cheapest*
Counterpoint	*Machine B costs 10% more but offers 30% higher performance*
Therefore	*Buy Machine B for its better price-performance ratio*

- Syllogism

General premise	*All companies that meet the 3 criteria can be acquired*
Particular case	*Company A satisfies all 3 criteria*
Conclusion	*Company A can be acquired*

The structure shapes the way
the audience receives the messages

A well-structured presentation is a sign of clear thinking. Correspondingly, the audience is able to distinguish the essential from the details, responds favourably to the flow of arguments, and remembers the important messages.

As we shall see in the next chapter, the presenter enjoys more control and flexibility in delivering a well-structured presentation.

5 Setting up a storyboard

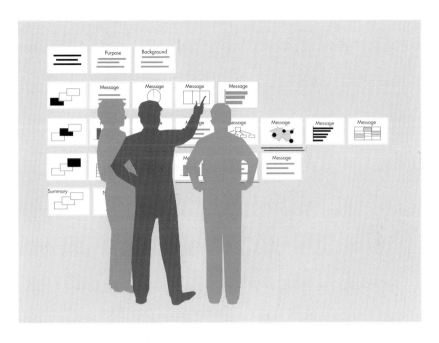

The storyboard is a powerful visual outlining tool

- **To organise ideas**
- **To check progress**
- **To work as a team**

The storyboard provides a visual outline of a presentation, just as a storyboard in advertising is used to visualise different proposals of for a new commercial.

Using a storyboard has several advantages. It enables you:

- *To organise ideas.* The storyboard gives a full view of the presentation at all times. The structure can be easily checked and new approaches tried out.

- *To check progress.* The storyboard shows how the presentation is progressing. At a glance, it is apparent what remains to be done.

- *To work as a team.* The storyboard provides a common reference for a team. They can use it to review the presentation at intervals, to divide up responsibilities and to ensure that the parts prepared by different members fit coherently.

Think early about
the presentation

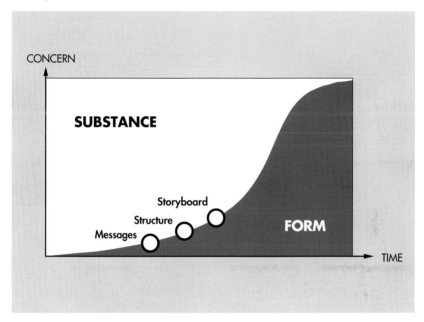

A key principle behind the storyboard approach is to start thinking early about the presentation and to build it up progressively. The presenter should not wait until he has "found the answer" before planning how to communicate the result.

A storyboard will guide you in the search for information and help you to approach the presentation from the audience's perspective.

Start by making hypotheses on the content and structure

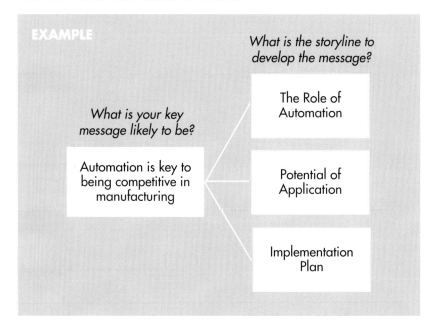

The best way to start is to imagine the end-result:

- Determine what your *key message* is likely to be, even if you do not have all the information necessary to decide on it. This will help you identify the information that supports or refutes your hypothesis.

- Imagine a *storyline* or scenario that best develops your key message. In other words, think about how you would structure your presentation in three parts.

Plan for the form of the presentation:
1. Duration...

How much time can your audience spare?	Presentation *30 mins* Discussion *20 mins*
How many visuals are necessary?	
How to allocate them by sections?	

The duration of a presentation is what your audience want to spend, not how much time *you* need. Split the time you are permitted between the presentation and the discussion:

- If you have to persuade an audience on a controversial subject, allocate enough time (e.g. 2/3rd of total time) for the discussion. Prepare additional "back-up" visuals to anticipate detailed questioning.

- If you simply want to inform a favourable audience, concentrate on the presentation and leave about 1/3rd of total time for any discussion.

Always plan to finish on time. Hardly anyone complains if a presentation is shorter than expected.

Plan for the form of the presentation:
2. Number of visuals...

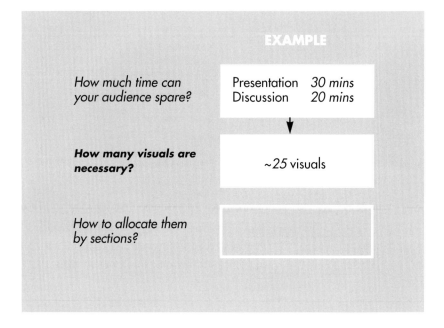

The number of visuals for a given duration of presentation depends on the complexity of the subject and the style of the speaker. As a rule of thumb, plan to speak for 1 to 1^1/$_2$ minutes on average per visual*. This ratio of the number of visuals may appear high, but:

- It forces the presenter to prepare simple visuals.

- The presentation is more dynamic because each new visual revives the audience's attention. Three visuals with three points each are better than one with nine points.

- The presenter has the flexibility to skip visuals to shorten the presentation.

When a presenter speaks beyond three minutes on a visual, he is no longer making a visual presentation but a speech.

*A 35mm slide or computer-driven presentation
 may contain even more visuals

Plan for the form of the presentation:
3. Allocating the visuals

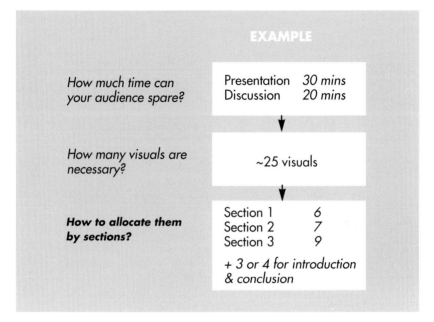

Reserve 3 to 4 visuals for the introduction and conclusion.

Allocate the remainder to each of the three sections. If one section turns out to be significantly longer than the other two, reconsider the structure.

Often, you will end up with more visuals than you can fit into the duration of the presentation. In that case you should retain what is absolutely necessary and keep the others aside for use in answering questions.

Set up a visual outline
of your presentation

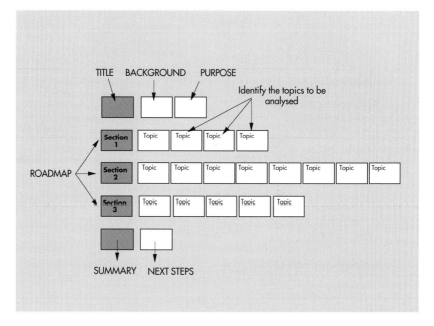

For long presentations prepared as a group, it is practical to set up a storyboard on a wall. This allows everyone to see and participate in the work.

Affix the required number of blank sheet of A4- or A5-sized paper on a wall. Each paper represents a visual. A row of sheets represents a section.

Include visuals that relate to the structure of the presentation:

- Introduction
- A roadmap for each section
- Conclusion

Mark on the top right corner of each sheet of paper, the topic you want to cover (e.g. market shares) even if you are not sure if the information is available.

Build the storyboard as you complete the analysis

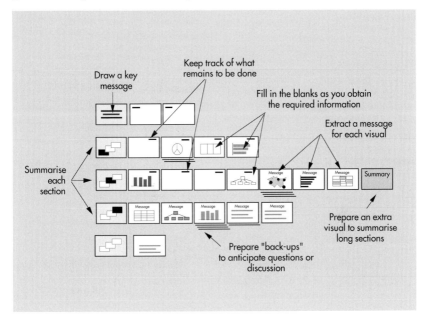

The storyboard serves as a flexible framework:

- Fill in or replace each blank sheet with relevant information as you complete your analysis. Insert or remove sheets as necessary to fill out or abridge the presentation. Prepare appropriate back-up visuals if you anticipate discussion on the details.

- Compose a message for each visual and write it on the top of each sheet. Then, consider the flow of the messages. Be prepared to rearrange their sequence, rephrase the messages, or insert/delete sheets to create a better flow.

- Summarise the contents at the end of each section. Finally draw an overall key message for the presentation.

Pay particular attention to the introduction and conclusion

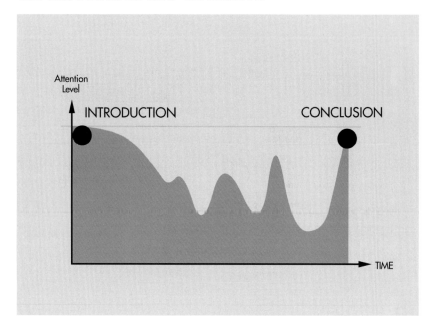

The audience's attention level is usually at its highest at the start of a presentation. The level drops away, fluctuates at various intervals and peaks again at the end. This curve varies from one audience to another and also depends on the topic covered and the talent of the speaker.

In some cases, the first thing the presenter must do is to establish his credibility. One technique is have someone introduce the presenter favourably before he makes the presentation. In addition, listing the sources of the information at the beginning may help to increase the audience's confidence in the content.

In every situation, we should take advantage of the two captive moments to communicate our strongest messages, to set expectations or create interest, and to lead them to take specific actions.

Prepare introductory visuals
for long presentations

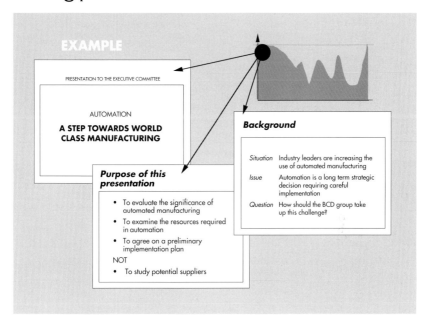

Write a title that captures attention

- Announce the *key message* to a neutral or positive audience. This direct approach can also be used to create a "shock" effect.
- Announce only the *subject* or *question* to a negative audience so that you can lead them towards your final conclusion.

Clarify the purpose of your presentation

Clarify what the audience can expect and how they will benefit. It is often useful also to state what is NOT your purpose.

Provide relevant background information

- *Situation-Issue-Problem* (as illustrated above)
- *Project schedule* showing where the project stands at the moment (e.g. with a GANTT chart)
- *Methodology* if the project is conducted according to a specific methodology.

Present a ROADMAP to show
how the contents are organised

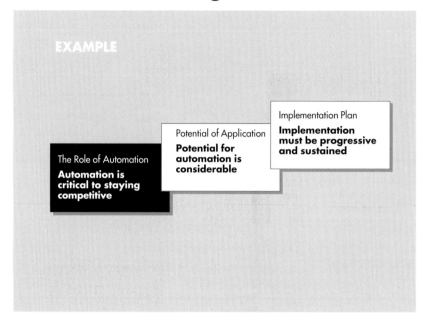

There is a well-known rule in communication: *"Say what you are going to say, say it, and say what you have said"*.

The roadmap displays the structure of your presentation at the outset:

- Use a diagram to show the different sections. You may incorporate creative designs that relate to the subject.

- Highlight the section you are about to present.

With the direct approach as illustrated above, present the conclusions of all the sections right at the beginning.

With the indirect approach, the roadmap reveals your conclusions step-by-step

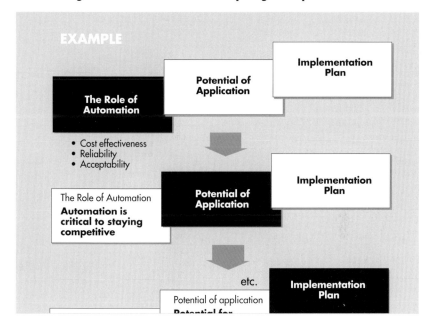

With the indirect approach, use the roadmaps to reveal the conclusions of each section progressively. The roadmap:

- explains in the beginning the three main topics covered in the presentation and launches the first section
- concludes a section by summarising what has just been presented. It then announces the next section to remind the audience of the new subject.
- summarises the whole presentation at the end by recapitulating the conclusions of all three sections.

The CONCLUSION
aims for tangible results

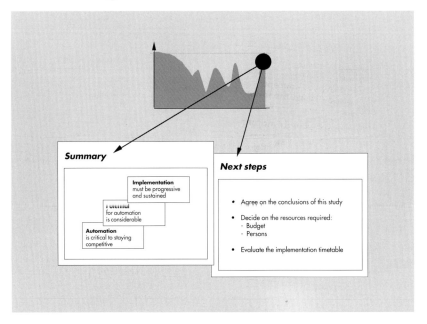

Summarise the whole presentation

Close the presentation strongly and memorably. Give a synopsis of the presentation by using the final roadmap to review the concluding messages of each section.

Propose the Next Steps

Launch the discussion by introducing the decisions or actions to be taken. This helps to direct the audience's attention and make the discussion more result-oriented. The last visual could be:

- an agenda of the ideas to be discussed and recommendations to be approved (as illustrated above)
- an action plan or GANTT chart describing the next steps of your project.

Next Steps are in fact what the presenter should aim to get out of the meeting. There is a saying: "If you want something, ask for it".

Review the messages
for consistency and flow

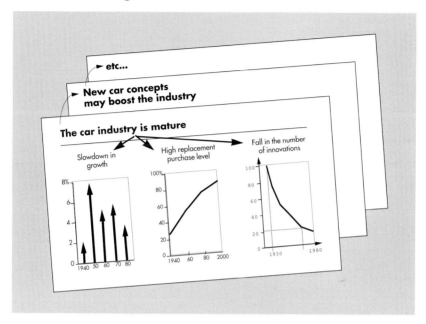

Check that the message on each visual is consistent with its supporting information. If you include several charts on the same visual, ensure that they support the same message (example above). If each of the charts requires detailed explanation, prepare a separate visual for each chart.

Check also that each message links logically to the next. If not, consider if you should rearrange their order, rewrite some of the messages, or even insert a new visual to bridge a gap in the sequence.

Add "milestones" to identify the position of each visual within the presentation

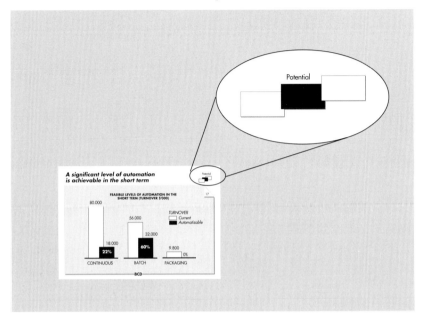

The listener is like a passenger on a journey. Even though he knows the way, he still needs markers now and then to check where he has reached along the way. Similarly, a milestone is a reminder of where each visual fits within the structure of the presentation.

Graphically, the milestone can be a miniature version of the roadmap positioned on the top right corner of the visual. The current section is highlighted and a short label identifies the topic. Alternatively, a milestone can simply state the topic without a graphic. The roadmaps themselves do not need a milestone.

If a section is long or complex, consider creating a sub-roadmap within the section. In this case, the milestone refers to this sub-roadmap. Do not display two milestones on the same visual.

Simplify your storyboard
for shorter presentations

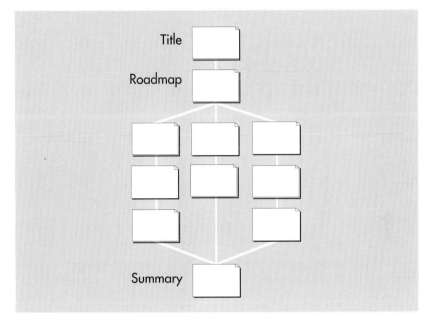

A short presentation (about 10 visuals) requires fewer visuals to show the structure. An overall title, one roadmap and a conclusion may be sufficient.

In such cases, the storyboard can be set up with Post-it™ stickers on a flip-chart and arranged vertically as shown above.

For simple presentations, set up the storyboard in the form of a "comic strip"

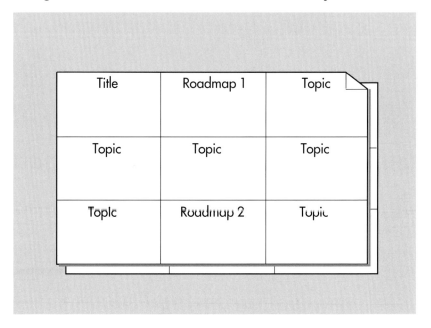

Another method of setting up the storyboard for a simple presentation is the "comic-strip".

Divide an A4- or A3-sized paper into several rectangles. Each rectangle represents a visual. However, this method has a constraint. It is difficult to try out different sequences or insert new visuals.

The completed storyboard serves as the draft for producing the visuals

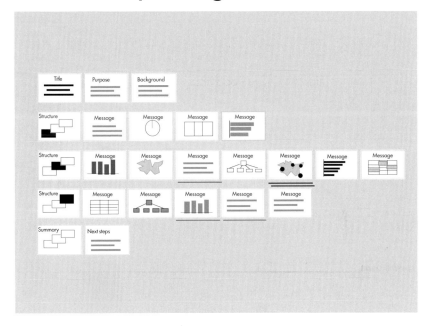

The final storyboard will in most cases look different from the one set up initially. The use of the storyboard avoids the typical practice of completing the analysis before transforming the results into a presentation at the last moment.

It is not necessary to wait until the storyboard is fully completed before starting to produce the visuals. You can gain time and avoid bottle-necks by starting to produce the visuals which appear ready. In this case, replace the draft on the wall with the produced visual. But be prepared to modify and redo them as your analysis progresses.

6 Designing Visual Aids

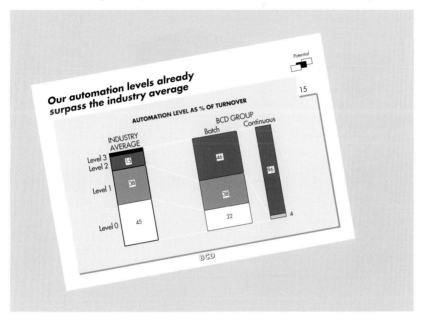

Define a graphic layout and visual style

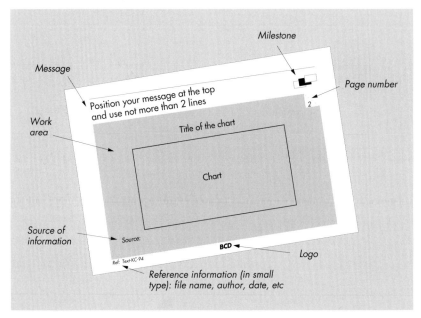

Maintain a consistent graphic layout and style throughout all your visuals. Pre-designed templates are available with presentation software. However, avoid those with elaborate designs and colours that divert attention from the content. A few rules and tips to note:

- *Choose a horizontal page setup* The bottom part of the screen is often too low and blocked by the projector.

- *Create a graphic work area* (with a frame boundary, lines or background colour) to focus the space in which you show your supporting information.

- *Determine the style*: i.e. position, fonts and sizes of information which will be repeated on each visual. In particular,
  - make messages prominent (e.g. 24 point bold)
  - texts must be of at least 18 point size
  - put non-essential information (logo, presentation title/reference, etc) at the bottom

Texts: A presentation is not a report projected on the screen

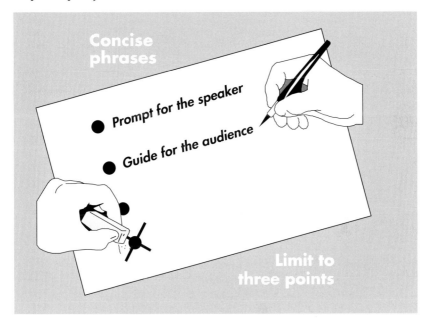

Texts in a visual fulfill two needs :

They prompt the speaker on the points that he has to elaborate.

They guide the audience on the points that will be covered and communicate the basic information if their attention wanders. If texts are long or complete, the audience is either turned off listening or turned off reading because the presenter's comments actually interfere with the reading.

Texts must therefore be concise and limited to three points.

Visual aids increase
the impact of presentations

- Listening and understanding of the audience is improved

- The ability to retain information is five times higher

- The speaker appears to be more professional and persuasive

- Consensus is reached more often by members in the meeting

- Meetings are one-third shorter in duration

In 1981, a well-known U.S. university conducted a study to evaluate the role of visual aids in business presentations.

The conclusions of this study are presented here in the form of a visual to serve as an example.

Write concisely...

- Listener understands better
- Speaker is more convincing
- Retention increases 5 times
- Consensus is more frequent
- Meetings are 1/3rd shorter

Short phrases attract attention and are more memorable:

- **Remove secondary information and unnecessary words**

  e.g. ~~Listening and~~ understanding is improved (understanding includes the process of listening). Also, Meetings are 1/3rd shorter ~~in duration~~.

- **Write in the active and direct form**

  Replace nouns with verbs e.g. ~~understanding~~ understand.

- **Express ideas in the same style.**

  e.g. Write the phrases or sentences in the same way (e.g. start all sentences with a verb)

In this example, we have reduced the number of words from 43 to 19 without losing the essence of the text.

...but do not
lose the idea

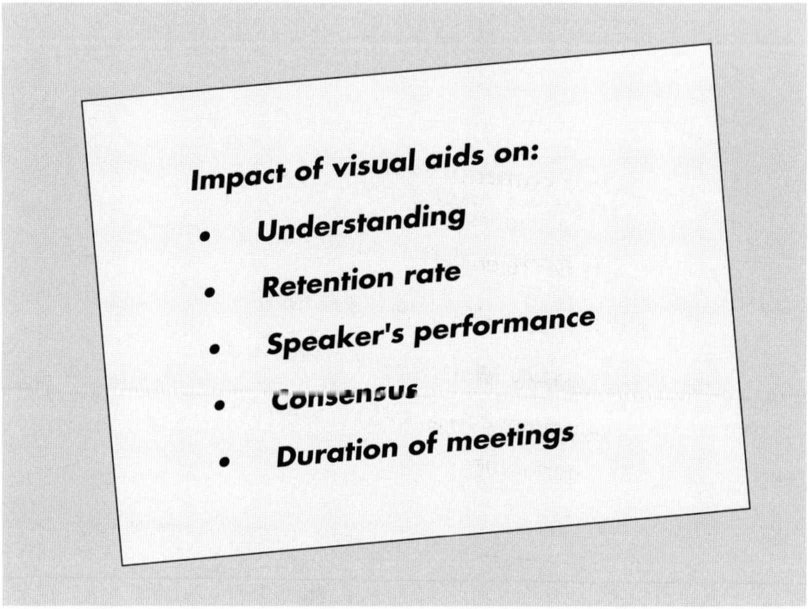

Impact of visual aids on:

- **Understanding**
- **Retention rate**
- **Speaker's performance**
- **Consensus**
- **Duration of meetings**

A concise text should still express an idea instead of just the topic. For example, texts should not be formulated as above.

Limit to three supporting ideas
by grouping the points...

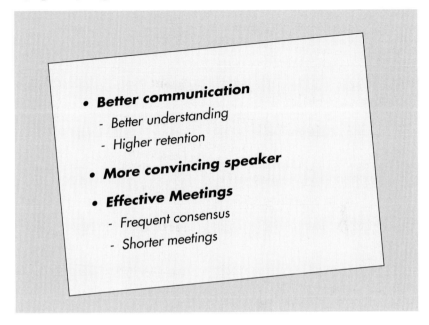

- **Better communication**
  - Better understanding
  - Higher retention
- **More convincing speaker**
- **Effective Meetings**
  - Frequent consensus
  - Shorter meetings

When presented with a list of the five conclusions as in this example, tests have regularly shown that most people can immediately recall only 2 or 3 items. Morever, the items remembered differ from one person to another.

Focus people's attention to the important ideas - limit yourself to three main points. One approach is to group the list as shown above. Often in a long list, some of the points are actually sub-points of another.

... or by selecting the most important points

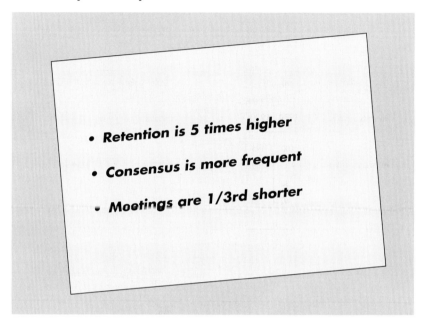

- Retention is 5 times higher
- Consensus is more frequent
- Meetings are 1/3rd shorter

Limiting to three key points prevents the audience from being distracted by the minor points. Select the points based on the interest of the audience.

- The example above addresses someone who is concerned about the efficiency of his team.

- On the other hand, a trainer may be more interested in:
    - *improved understanding*
    - *5 times better retention*
    - *more convincing speaker*

If an audience is not convinced by the three strongest arguments, adding two weaker ones would be equally ineffective. In fact, a conclusion which is supported by so many arguments can appear suspect. Moreover, the negative audience has greater opportunity to challenge your reasoning.

Graphics:
A chart reveals more than numbers

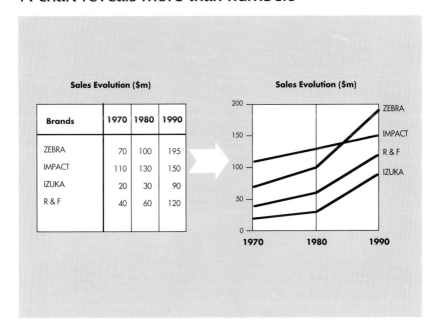

Study the numbers in the table on the left and try to extract a message. It requires concentration and effort.

With the chart on the right, the audience sees immediately the relationships between the lines. At a glance, one can draw several messages, e.g.

"All brands enjoyed growth"

"Impact did not keep up with competitive growth"

"Zebra has outpaced the competition to become No. 1"

Graphics make information easier to understand and remember. Close your eyes. You can still visualise the shape of the four lines. Now, try recalling the numbers...

When designing visuals, remember the words of Herodotus: "The ear is a less trustworthy witness than the eye"

The purpose of graphics is to support the message

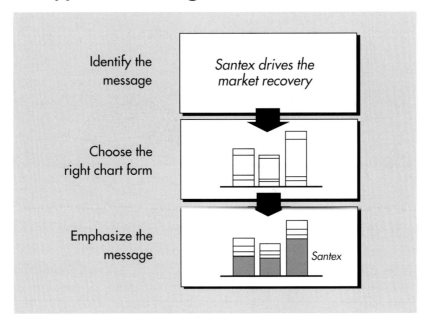

To create effective graphics:

1. Identify the message

A set of numbers contain many messages. The appropriate chart depends on the message to be expressed. So, the first step is to identify the message you wish to communicate with the data.

2. Choose the right chart form

The library of chart forms is vast. Each chart form carries an inherent "visual" message. The best chart is one which reinforces or explains the message. An appendix to the book describes some of more commonly used chart forms and the types of messages for which they are appropriate.

3. Emphasize the message

Focus the audience's attention quickly to what is important. This can be achieved visually with the creative use of colour, shading, typeface, arrows, lines, etc.

Different messages can be drawn from a neutral chart

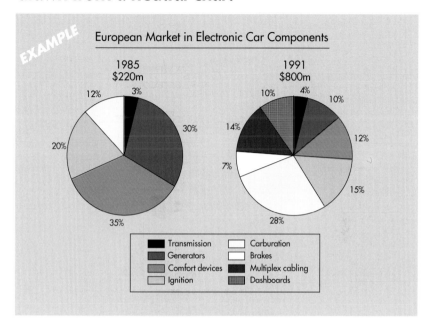

European Market in Electronic Car Components

1985
$220m

1991
$800m

Legend:
- Transmission
- Generators
- Comfort devices
- Ignition
- Carburation
- Brakes
- Multiplex cabling
- Dashboards

The charts above shows in a raw form the composition of the market. They can communicate several different messages, such as:

- The market quadrupled in 6 years

- In 1991, new applications account for 30% of the market

- New applications represent 30% of an enlarged market

- Share for comfort devices was reduced by 3 times

Use of a neutral chart runs the risk that the audience may draw a conclusion which is different from the one you want to get across.

For example, consider how we can illustrate the first two messages.

Design a chart that supports the message

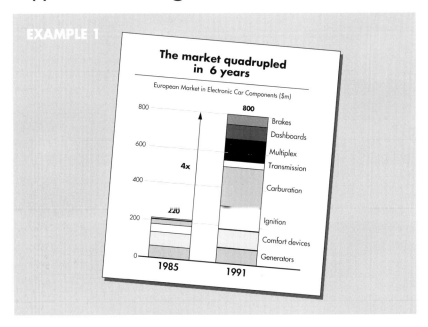

The market quadrupled in 6 years

European Market in Electronic Car Components ($m)

800		800
		Brakes
		Dashboards
600		
		Multiplex
	4x	Transmission
400		
		Carburation
	220	
200		Ignition
		Comfort devices
0		Generators
	1985	1991

Comparison :   Time series evolution

Chart Form :   Segmented columns in value

Adding value: Use grey shadings to differentiate the segments.

Rank segments in decreasing size from the bottom.

Group new applications at the top and shade them in darker greys.

Place an arrow to highlight the 4x increase.

Place the labels next to the segments instead of using a legend which is difficult to read.

74

Design a chart that supports the message

EXAMPLE 2

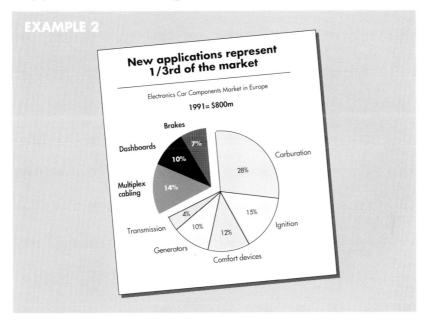

New applications represent 1/3rd of the market

Electronics Car Components Market in Europe

1991= $800m

Comparison :   Composition

Chart Form :   Pie chart

Adding value: Group the new applications and detach them slightly from the pie.

Shade the new applications in darker greys and use bold types for the labels.

Rank the other segments in increasing size from 12 noon.

QUANTITATIVE charts
compare values

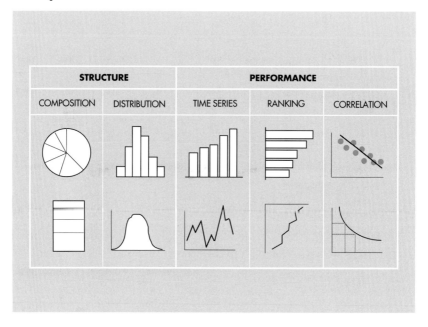

STRUCTURE		PERFORMANCE		
COMPOSITION	DISTRIBUTION	TIME SERIES	RANKING	CORRELATION

A value is meaningful only when compared with other values. Charts depict such comparisons and these can be classified into:

Structural comparisons

- *Composition* shows the relative importance of the components of a whole

- *Distribution* shows a population broken down into quantitative ranges

Performance comparisons

- *Time series* show how performance varies over time
- *Ranking charts* compare performances of various items
- *Correlation* shows the relationship between two or more variables

See appendix for illustrations of basic and extended chart forms for each of these comparisons.

Diagrams illustrate
QUALITATIVE information

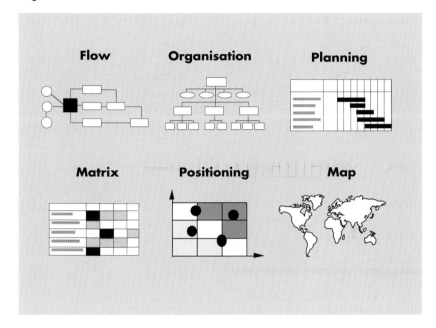

Qualitative diagrams symbolize conceptual relationships and their range is limitless. Above are examples of the more common diagrams:

- *Flow* describes a process
- *Organisation* chart represents the operational and functional structure
- *Planning* chart lists the actions to be achieved (what, who, when)
- *Matrix* evaluates performance against a set of criteria
- *Positioning* map visualises the relative position of an item in a conceptual grid
- *Maps* indicate geographic positions combined with flows or quantitative data

See appendix for an illustration of the use of each diagram.

7 Presenting with visual aids

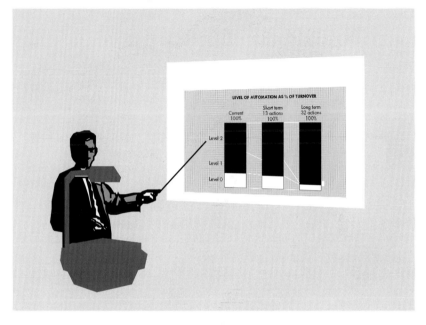

A good presentation is more than just a speech with visuals

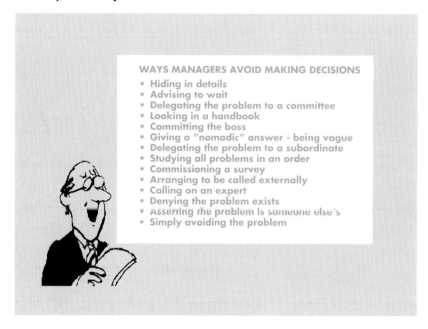

A good speaker is not automatically a good presenter. Presenting with visuals involves different skills to speech-making. Incorrectly used, visuals become more of a hindrance than an aid.

Practice and planning are the only way to ensure that you get the most out of your presentation. The effective presenter:

- rehearses
- prepares the stage

The conscientious presenter
rehearses at least three times

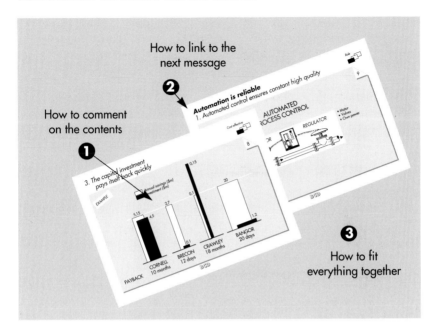

How to link to the next message

How to comment on the contents

How to fit everything together

Confidence comes from practice. That means rehearsing at least three times:

1. **Master the contents**
   Go through each visual and practise how to comment on its content (e.g. finding an example).

2. **Create a flow**
   Prepare for a smooth transition between visuals. Two simple techniques: Identify the link to the next visual (e.g. ...on the contrary...) or put forth a rhetorical question which introduces the next subject/message. Jot a few key words on the flaps of the transparency holder as an aide-mémoire.

3. **Fit everything together**
   The third rehearsal is a simulated presentation, if possible, in front of a mock audience. It also allows you to check if the presentation finishes on time.

Make the venue conducive
for a presentation

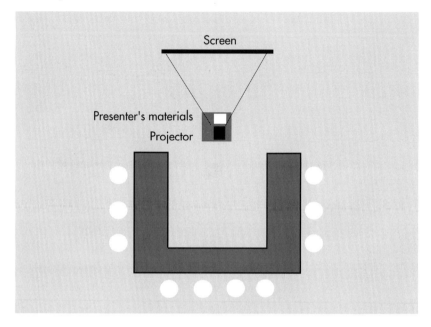

Do not accept a venue as it is set up. The presenter should consider re-arranging an unsuitable setting.

- *Set up a U-shaped seating plan* if feasible. It facilitates face to face contact with each audience. Also, the screen is unobstructed from most angles.

- *Remove unnecessary fixtures* (e.g. table, podium) which act as a physical barrier between the presenter and the audience. The space in front should be uncluttered. Use a small table to place the overhead projecter and presentation materials.

- *Check all equipment & materials* (e.g. flip charts, markers, pointer). Interrupting a presentation to set up/adjust equipment or to search for materials is disruptive and irritating for the audience.

Choose where to stand and move deliberately

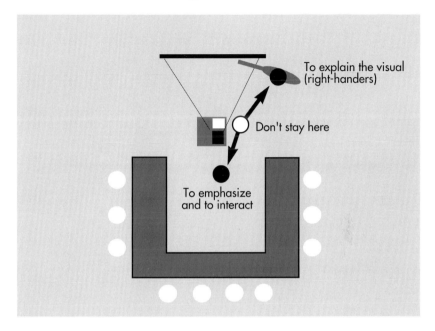

To explain the visual (right-handers)

Don't stay here

To emphasize and to interact

Position

Stand next to the screen to explain a visual with a pointer or using the hand. But do not speak towards the screen with your back to the audience. Some prefer to point on the projector. If you do so, avoid looking down at the projector. While speaking, place a pen on the projector and move to the side to speak so that the audience can see the screen.

Movement

Move to the centre of the stage now and then to emphasize a point, to answer a question, and to encourage interaction.

Guide the audience
through the visual

1 Quality is the single most important purchase
criterion for our target client base

CRITERIA	Age groups					
	15-19	20-29	30-39	40-49	50-59	+60
Price	●	●	●	●	●	●
Quality	●	•	●	●	●	●
Packaging	●	●	●	●	●	
Credit	●	●	•	•	●	●
Image	●	•	●	●	●	●
Appearance	•	●	●	●	•	•
After-sales Service	•	•	•	●	●	●
Fashion	●	●	•	•	•	

2

Importance

Low ●
Medium ●
High ●

3

Introduce the visual before showing it

In a few words, explain the link from the previous visual, or put a
rhetorical question which introduces the new topic (e.g. *"What are our
consumers' purchase criteria?"*) . The audience then knows what to
expect and is thus better prepared to receive the message.

Show the visual

Give the audience a moment to scan its content (e.g. as you move to
the screen).

Comment methodically on the visual

1. Announce the message as it is written on the visual or in slightly
   different words.

2. Give a quick overview of what the chart is about (e.g. in the
   example above, explain the two axes and the legend).

3. Highlight the important points. A common error is to rush too
   quickly to a detail on the visual.

Vary the rhythm and medium to maintain interest

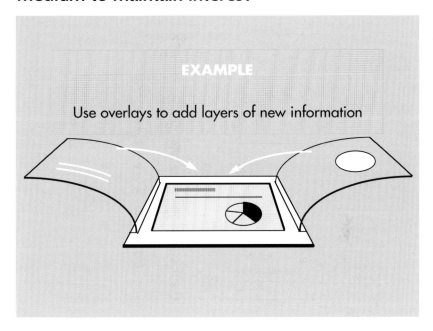

EXAMPLE

Use overlays to add layers of new information

Use overlays to avoid showing too much information at once. This technique is most effective with a computer-driven presentation.

Switch off the projector to draw attention to yourself when you are not explaining a visual (e.g. during the introduction, when answering a question).

Mask part of a visual. However, audiences normally dislike this practice and can even be distracted by what is "hidden". To use this technique effectively, show the whole visual before covering part of it. Alternatively, use a darkly-coloured or grey transparent mask so that the audience can still see vaguely what is covered.

Create events at appropriate moments
- Change the medium (flip chart, video, samples)
- Give an unexpected break
- Switch presenters
- Introduce a discussion or exercise

Choose the
appropriate medium

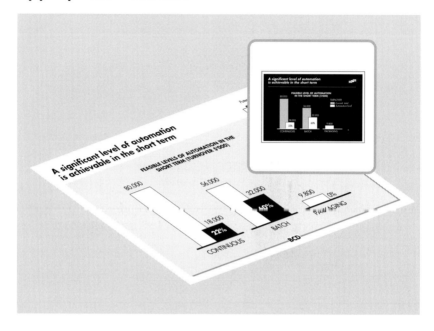

The two most popular media for presentation are:

Transparencies

This remains the most commonly used medium. Transparencies are easy to produce and are effective even under bright lights. The presenter has the flexibility of being able to remove, rearrange or retrieve transparencies. They are ideal for working meetings involving a small to medium-sized audience.

35mm slides

These are especially attractive with colour pictures but take longer to produce (and modify). To have impact, they need to be shown under dimmed lighting. As the presenter's contact with the audience is less direct, 35mm slides are best used for large audiences where the main purpose is to inform and impress.

Multi-media "shows" offer more features but can be distracting

The present trend is towards computer-driven multi-media presentations using LCD panels and projectors.

This method has several advantages over transparencies. Firstly, there is no need to print the visuals thereby facilitating last minute changes. Secondly, the presenter can build a complex chart by adding new elements of information gradually. Finally, the presentation can include animation and sound.

In using these devices, keep the following in mind:

· Do not let the medium become the focus of the audience's interest.

· Use more graphics. Text is more tiring to read due to the lower resolution and brightness of the projected image.

· Check well ahead of time that the equipment works.

Prepare a handout
for the audience

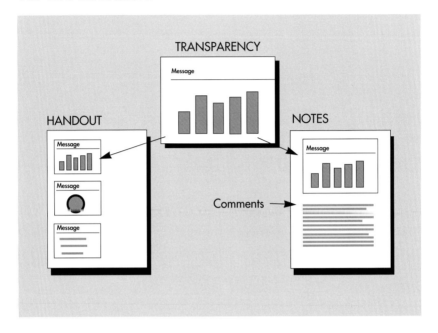

Most audiences will ask for a copy of your presentation. However, do not distribute the copy before the presentation. With a handout during the presentation, the audience normally flips through the pages and reads ahead rather than listen. Also, you confuse the audience should you decide to skip a few visuals. However, handouts can be useful during the presentation when the audience is a small group working on a complex subject,

In addition to full-size transparencies, most presentation software print:

Handouts with 2 to 8 miniature visuals on a page. This format is useful if you have to hand out a copy before the presentation. As the visuals are difficult to read, the audience is encouraged to listen. There are few pages to turn and the audience can make notes in the margins.

Speaker Notes Originally intended to assist the speaker in preparing his comments, they can also serve as an "intelligent" handout for the audience. They also replace the need for a written report.

For your notes:

For your notes:

EXAMPLE OF A
PRESENTATION STORYBOARD

A fictitious presentation on "Automation - A step towards world class manufacturing" is used here to demonstrate the methods described in this book.

The following double page shows the completed storyboard. The reader should concentrate on the form rather than on the content of the presentation. Each visual is then reproduced in subsequent pages with relevant comments.

Example **91**

Introduction

 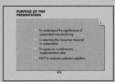 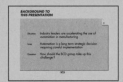

Section 1

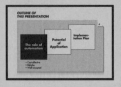 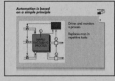 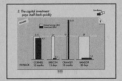

Section 2

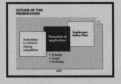  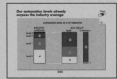 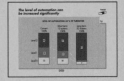

Section 3

 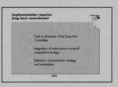 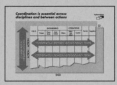 

Conclusion

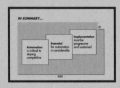 

PRESENTATION STORYBOARD

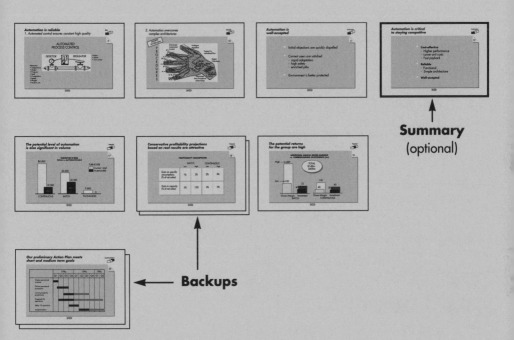

Summary
(optional)

Backups

Example **93**

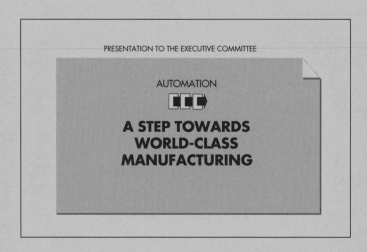

AUTOMATION

**A STEP TOWARDS
WORLD-CLASS
MANUFACTURING**

Title *With the direct approach, this first visual states the concluding message. If you know that this message will provoke negative response from the audience, use the indirect approach by announcing only the subject or question, and revealing the key message at the end.*

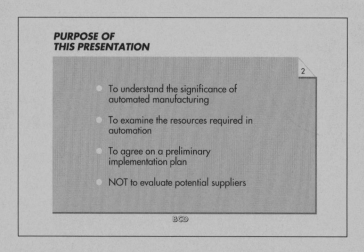

PURPOSE OF
THIS PRESENTATION

2

● To understand the significance of
automated manufacturing

● To examine the resources required in
automation

● To agree on a preliminary
implementation plan

● NOT to evaluate potential suppliers

BCD

Purpose *This is to set expectations and to ensure that the audience understands the scope and issues underlying the presentation.*
Stating your purpose also discourages the audience from raising questions which are out of context.

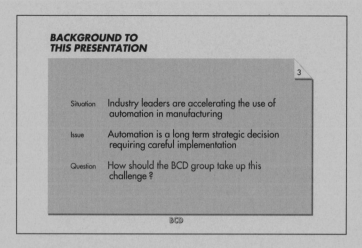

BACKGROUND TO THIS PRESENTATION

3

Situation — Industry leaders are accelerating the use of automation in manufacturing

Issue — Automation is a long term strategic decision requiring careful implementation

Question — How should the BCD group take up this challenge ?

BCD

Background *With a new or poorly-informed audience, explain the context of the presentation.*

Describe briefly the general situation, the problem encountered, and the question that is raised.

If the presentation is part of a project, show a planning chart to remind the audience of the progress achieved.

Example **95**

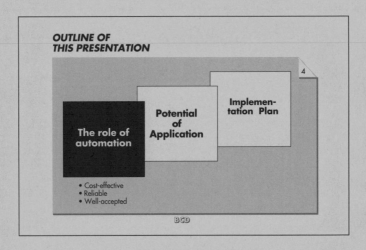

Roadmap *Use it to introduce each section.*

Highlight the section you are about to present. Also announce the main sub-topics covered in the section.

The messages covered in this section are mostly factual statements.

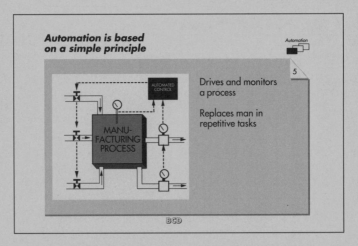

*The roadmap is reproduced in miniature in the upper right corner. This is a **milestone** to remind the audience where each visual fits into the presentation.*

Shade the current section and add the topic being presented. Place it in the same position on each visual.

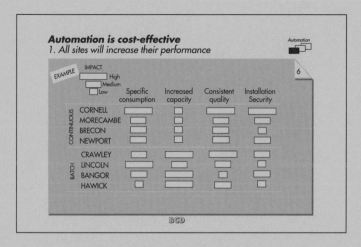

A title may sometimes contain two levels.

The first line in bold type introduces a main point within this section.

The second line is the message of the visual.

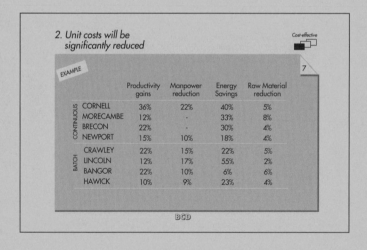

Example **97**

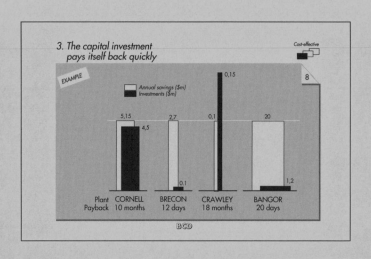

3. The capital investment pays itself back quickly

Cost-effective

EXAMPLE

8

■ Annual savings ($m)
□ Investments ($m)

	5,15	2,7	0,15		0,1		20	

CORNELL 4,5
BRECON 0.1
CRAWLEY 0,1
BANGOR 1,2

Plant   CORNELL   BRECON   CRAWLEY   BANGOR
Payback 10 months 12 days   18 months 20 days

BCD

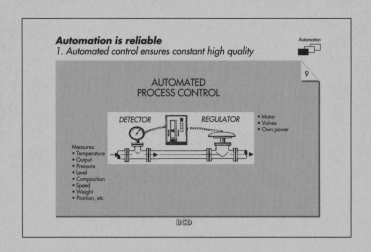

Automation is reliable
1. Automated control ensures constant high quality

Automation

9

AUTOMATED
PROCESS CONTROL

DETECTOR   REGULATOR
• Motor
• Valves
• Own power

Measures:
• Temperature
• Output
• Pressure
• Level
• Composition
• Speed
• Weight
• Position, etc.

BCD

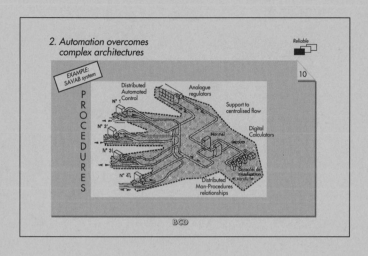

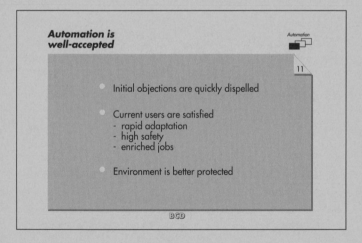

Before creating the visuals, decide on the font styles and sizes for the message, sub-title, bullet points and other texts.

Use the same style throughout. From time to time, a different font style may be used to stress a particular point.

Example **99**

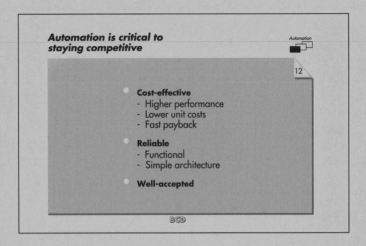

For a long section, it may be useful to summarise it with a visual.

For a short section, summarise it directly using the roadmap as shown in the next visual.

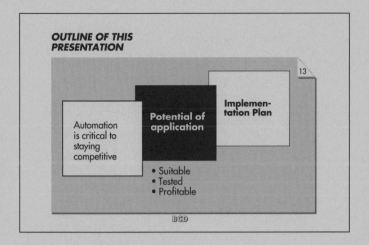

OUTLINE OF THIS
PRESENTATION

13

Automation
is critical to
staying
competitive

Potential of
application

Implemen-
tation Plan

• Suitable
• Tested
• Profitable

BCD

Show the **Roadmap** again.

Summarise the first section by replacing the subject with the conclusion.

Highlight the second section and announce the main points which will be covered.

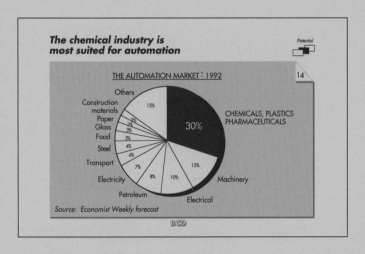

The chemical industry is
most suited for automation

Potential

THE AUTOMATION MARKET – 1992

14

Others
Construction
materials   15%
Paper   2%
Glass   2%
Food   3%   30%
Steel   4%
         4%
Transport
         7%
Electricity   8%   10%
Petroleum
                Electrical

CHEMICALS, PLASTICS
PHARMACEUTICALS

12%

Machinery

Source: Economist Weekly forecast

BCD

Change the milestone to show the new section.

The second section is highlighted with a new topic reference.

Example 101

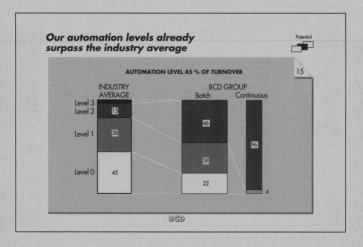

Use graphics creatively.

In this example, the greys become stronger to indicate increasing complexity of automation. The width of the columns is used to represent the volume.

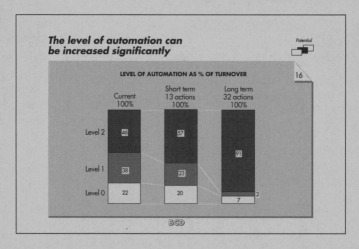

Notice that messages in this section are increasingly opinions.

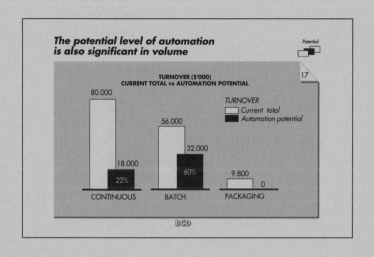

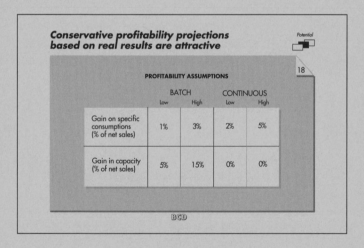

Be prepared with backup visuals containing more details. Do not present these backups initially but use them to answer questions or for discussion. Tell the audience that the details are available.

Example **103**

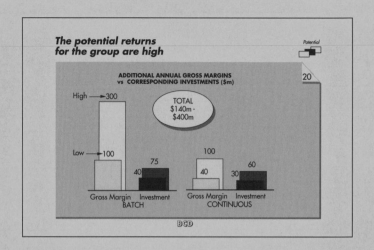

The potential returns
for the group are high

Potential

ADDITIONAL ANNUAL GROSS MARGINS
vs CORRESPONDING INVESTMENTS ($m)

20

High ➤ 300

TOTAL
$140m -
$400m

Low ➤ 100

100

75

40

40

60

30

Gross Margin   Investment
BATCH

Gross Margin   Investment
CONTINUOUS

BCD

104

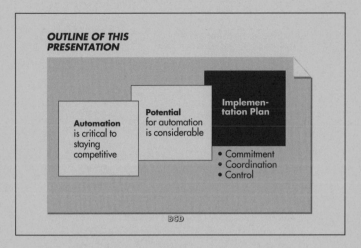

*Show the **Roadmap** again to summarise the current section and introduce the next.*

The topic of the second section also becomes a concluding message and the third section is now highlighted.

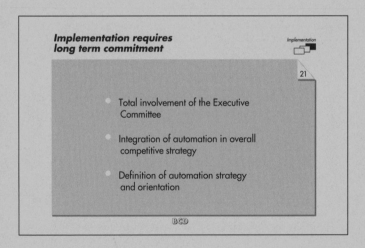

Again, the milestone is changed.

Notice that the messages in this final section are mostly recommendations.

Example 105

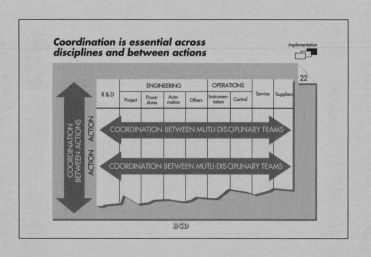

Coordination is essential across disciplines and between actions

Implementation

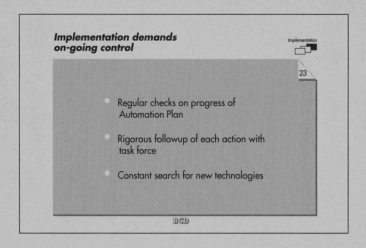

Implementation demands on-going control

Implementation

- Regular checks on progress of Automation Plan

- Rigorous followup of each action with task force

- Constant search for new technologies

BCD

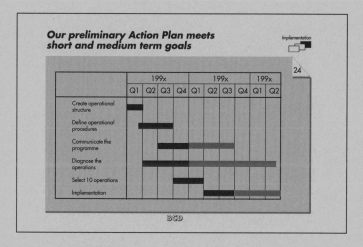

Close the presentation with something tangible and oriented towards the future.

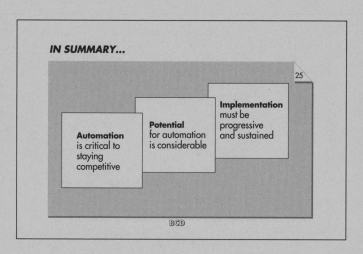

The final roadmap summarises the whole presentation.

We have moved from an outline with three topics in the beginning to a summary with three concluding storyline messages.

Example **107**

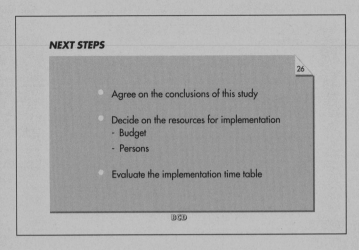

NEXT STEPS

26

- Agree on the conclusions of this study

- Decide on the resources for implementation
  - Budget
  - Persons

- Evaluate the implementation time table

BCD

Propose an agenda for the discussion. Be specific and precise as to what you want to achieve.

It focuses the discussion and directs the audience towards your objectives in making the presentation.

FINAL NOTE

The storyboard approach allows you to shorten the presentation at the very last moment.

For example :

- *If you have about 10 seconds, present the first visual with the key message.*

- *If you have less than a minute, present the key message and the summary of the three sections (i.e. visual 25).*

- *If you have about five minutes, present the key message, the summary and add a few key visuals from each section (i.e. visuals 12, 19 and 24) to support your conclusions.*

Example   **109**

QUANTITATIVE charts
compare values

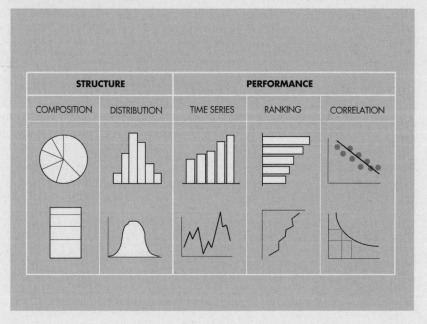

COMPOSITION shows how the parts make up the total

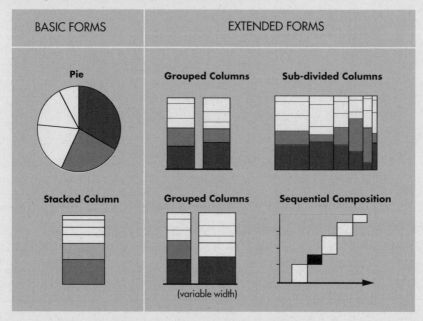

BASIC FORMS	EXTENDED FORMS

Pie

Grouped Columns

Sub-divided Columns

Stacked Column

Grouped Columns

Sequential Composition

(variable width)

Composition shows the relative sizes of the components of the whole. The basic chart forms are:

Pie chart
- Start at 12 'o clock and rank segments in decreasing size clockwise. Limit to 7/8 segments.
- Express in % rather than in value. Place the % inside the segments and the names next to the segments.
- Highlight the pertinent segment(s) with shading, colour, etc.

Stacked column
- Position the largest segment on the base line and rank the other segments in decreasing size. Limit to 7/8 segments.
- The rules of pie charts also generally apply here.

Pie charts and stacked columns can be used interchangeably to have more variety in a presentation.

The derived or extended forms are:

Grouped columns

If you need to compare several compositions, use stacked columns instead of pie charts. It is easier to compare the segments across columns. Moreover, there is no need for a legend or to repeat the segment labels for each pie. The width of each column can also be varied to represent the relative sizes of the compositions.

Sub-divided columns

They are used to illustrate two internal compositions: the column width along the horizontal axis shows one composition (e.g. share of total sales held by each region) and the segments in each column represent another composition (e.g. competitive shares held by individual brands within each region).

Sequential composition

This is a segmented column in which the segments are sequentially shifted to the right to portray chronological steps. For example, this chart could show how the cost of a product is built up along each step in the production process.

DISTRIBUTION shows a whole decomposed into quantitative ranges

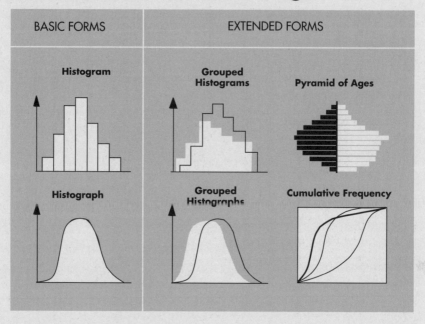

BASIC FORMS	EXTENDED FORMS
Histogram	Grouped Histograms / Pyramid of Ages
Histograph	Grouped Histographs / Cumulative Frequency

Distribution can illustrate, for example, the number of employees in different salary bands. The basic chart forms are:

Histogram
- Limit the number of bands to 15. If more, turn it into a histograph by smoothing the profile.
- Use the same range for each column, except for the two ends to shorten the series.
- Indicate the % at the top of each column. If necessary, the vertical axis can indicate the value.

Histograph
- Display a few key values on the horizontal axis.
- Show the vertical axis in %.

The extended forms are:

Grouped histograms

compare two histograms, e.g. salary distribution of company A vs B. To facilitate comparison, represent one distribution in grey and the other by an outline.

Grouped histographs

compare up to three histographs. The curves must be clearly contrasted to allow easy comparison.

Pyramid of ages

is used to compare the profile of age ranges between two groups of population (e.g. male and female) or the same population over two periods.

Cumulative frequency

serves to illustrate concentration (e.g. the Pareto 80:20 principle) or "skew".

TIME SERIES shows how performance varies over time

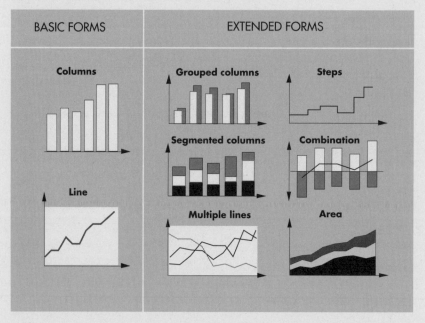

BASIC FORMS	EXTENDED FORMS
Columns	Grouped columns / Steps
Line	Segmented columns / Combination
	Multiple lines / Area

Columns

Columns are better than lines at displaying change in *value*, e.g.: *The market has increased 40% in 6 years.*

- Limit number of columns to about 10. The space between the columns should be different (smaller) than the column width to prevent uncomfortable optical "vibrating" effect.
- Place values at the head of columns.
- Write the dates with only 2 digits (e.g. '94) to prevent overcrowding of the chart.
- Ensure that the columns reflect *regular* intervals on the horizontal time scale.
- Highlight any change if appropriate with arrows and texts.
- Break the columns at the base if the vertical scale does not begin at zero.

Line charts

Lines are better at showing fluctuations or trends over long periods when the absolute values are less important, e.g. *The market has increased steadily at 6% since 1980.*

- Use vertical axis for the values. Beware of the effect of using different scales (arithmetic, logarithmic, index), and of breaking the scale on the slope of the line.
- Add relevant figures at significant points on the line.
- Draw thin grids to help the audience see the fluctuations.

Grouped columns

They compare how two or three series evolve over the same period. Overlap each pair of columns slightly to contrast the differences.

Segmented columns

Maintain the order of the segments. Alternate between light and dark shadings. Rank segments from the bottom if this is relevant.

Multiple lines

Also known as a sphagetti chart. Limit to 5 or 6 lines and contrast them with colour or different shades for easier comparison.

Steps

They show the evolution of a variable which moves at irregular intervals e.g. interest rates.

Combination columns/lines

The columns above show positive values and the ones below negative values. The line shows the net difference. A second line can be added to show the cumulative balance. Examples: trade balances (exports, imports and net) , cash flow, profit/loss.

Area or surface

An area represents many segmented columns over a long time period. Joining the columns and segments as a surface makes it easier to read. Example: Age composition of a population over 50 years.

RANKING compares the performance of several items

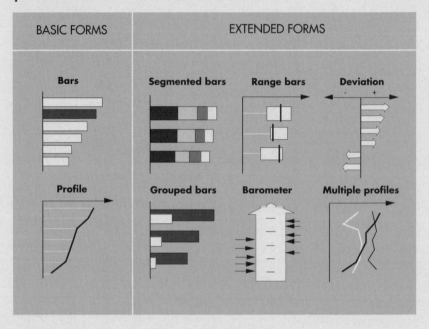

BASIC FORMS	EXTENDED FORMS
Bars	Segmented bars Range bars Deviation
Profile	Grouped bars Barometer Multiple profiles

Bars

Many users do not appreciate the difference between bars (horizontal) and columns (vertical), and therefore use them interchangeably. Columns read from left to right to connote a time flow. They should be used to express a *time* series. Bars read from top to bottom to indicate *ranking* at a point in time.

- Limit to 10-12 items and rank them on performance (sometimes the shorter bars indicate better performance).

- Label the names of the items on the left and the value on the right.

- Highlight one or several bars which are relevant to the message.

Profile

A profile rates the performance of an item along several criteria on a scale, e.g. importance of different purchase criteria for a consumer.

- Rank the criteria in decreasing order of importance, unless there is an imposed order (chronology, size, etc.).
- Use a scale (e.g. 1 to 5) and trace fine gridlines on the chart.
- Place the labels for the criteria on the left.

Segmented bars & grouped bars

Graphic rules are similar to those for segmented and grouped columns.

Range bars

Each bar shows the maximum/minimum range of values, e.g. the range of salaries paid across different professions. A vertical mark on the bar could indicate the average of that bar, and a line across the chart could show the overall average.

Barometer

A barometer is more effective than bars to compare many (e.g. >10) items. Set up a scale in the middle. Split the items into two groups (left and right) and position each item against the scale. Example: Penetration of cable TV in European versus other countries.

Deviation bars

Deviation or sliding bars show the change of several items from one period to another, e.g. increase (right side) or decrease (left side) in number of cars registered for different brands.

Multiple profiles

Several profiles evaluated on the same criteria can be drawn on the same chart to facilitate comparison, e.g. our performance versus competition; performance in 1994 versus 1993.

CORRELATION compares performance along 2 or more dimensions

BASIC FORMS	EXTENDED FORMS

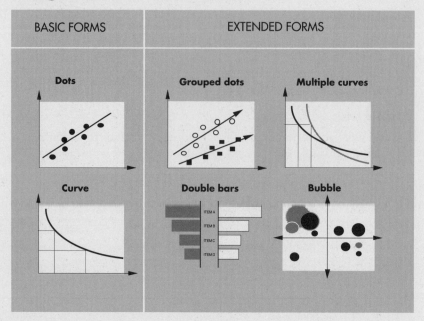

Correlation demonstrates how closely 2 or more dimensions are inter-related, e.g. discount offered and resulting sales increase.

Dots or **Scatter**

- Use the horizontal axis for the *independent* variable (e.g. discount offered), the vertical axis for the *dependent* variable (e.g. sales increase).

- Write the name of each dot if there is enough space. If not, indicate the more important ones.

- Draw a line of closest fit or a broad grey shading to highlight the correlation.

Curves

Curves demonstrate a mathematical correlation, e.g. the unit cost versus production volume. Respect the same graphic rules as for dots. Trace a few lines to illustrate the effect of the correlation.

Grouped dots

Sometimes, a scattering of dots reveal 2 or more separate correlations when we introduce another dimension, e.g. the correlation between discount offered and sales increase is not similar for *luxury* and *commodity* items.

Double bars

Use double bars if there are only a few items. Place the name of the items in the centre and rank the bars according to the more important or the independent dimension.

Multiple curves

Emphasize the reference curve, e.g. *current* production cost compared with that obtainable with new equipment.

Bubbles

A bubble chart adds a third dimension to a dot chart by varying the size of the dots. Use the horizontal and vertical axes for the more important dimensions and the area of the bubbles to indicate the weight of the item, e.g. for a branded consumer product:

X axis :	Advertising expenditure
Y axis :	Unit sales price
Bubble size :	Sales volume (size of brand)

Be aware that it is difficult to compare the size of circles.

A fourth dimension can also be introduced by changing the shading or colour of the bubbles e.g. *international* vs *local* brands.

Diagrams illustrate
QUALITATIVE information

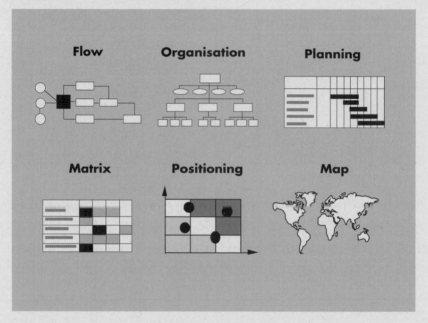

FLOW charts describe a physical or conceptual process

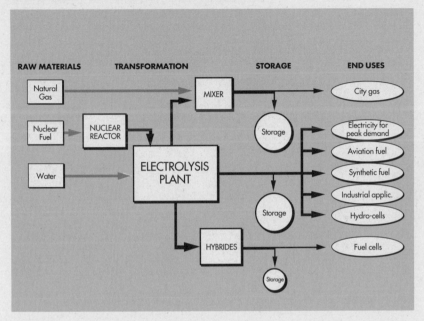

The flow chart above illustrates how hydrogen is industrially produced and its uses.

- Simplify the chart by grouping minor operations into main fields
- Organise activities in a sequential or chronological order
- Differentiate main groups of activity with different shapes
- Vary the size of the boxes according to the importance of the activity and not to the amount of text it contains
- Vary the thickness of the lines to indicate the importance of the flow
- Vary the style of lines (dotted, grey, etc) to indicate a different type of flow (information, material, etc)

ORGANISATION charts display functional and operational structures

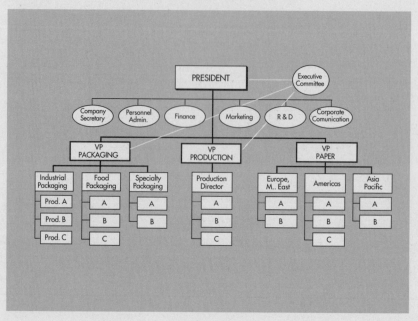

An organisation chart identifies each element in the organisation, its relative position and their relationship.

- Differentiate the nature of activity graphically, e.g. rectangles for operational entities, ovals for functions, and circles for committees.

- Vary the style of the connecting lines to differentiate the nature of the link between entities e.g. thick solid lines for hierarchical reporting and thin/dotted lines for functional relationships.

- Reduce the size of the boxes as you descend the organisation. Do not fix the size of the box to fit the text.

- Display the links for lower levels vertically to save space.

PLANNING charts answer
What? Who? When?

	Action
	Preparation
	○ Presentations

PHASES / ACTIVITIES	RESPONSIBILITIES			TIMING						
	JPK KN	JPM RRR	KC MD	F	M	A	M	J	J	A
1 - INDUSTRY ANALYSIS										
- Business system	✓				■					
- Generic Strategies	✓	✓		▬	■		12			
- Key Success Factors	✓	✓	✓		■		○			
2 - COMPANY ANALYSIS										
- Company strategy		✓	✓		■					
- Strength & weaknesses	✓	✓				▬	■	30		
- Key issues	✓	✓	✓				■	○		
3 - ISSUE ANALYSIS										
- Evaluation of issues	✓	✓							■	
- Recommendations	✓	✓	✓						■	
- Action Plan		✓	✓						■	31 ○

A planning chart, also called a GANTT chart, shows a list of activities or actions, the persons responsible and the time table.

- Group the activities by major phases (in time or by objective) to simplify the chart.

- Express each activity with an active verb and describe the desired output to make the activities more result-oriented.

- Identify who is responsible for what.

- Show the duration of the activity with a bar which covers the period concerned.

- Distinguish the nature of the activities with different patterns, e.g. a grey bar or dotted lines for preparation and a dark bar for implementation.

- Indicate events such as meetings and decision points with a symbol (dot, circle, etc).

A MATRIX evaluate performance against a set of criteria

KEY: High (black) — Medium (grey) — Low (white)

SUITABILITY OF TEACHING METHODS

REQUIREMENT OF COURSE TOPIC	Case study	Group projects	Role playing	Reading	Lectures
Analyse problems	High	High	Low	Low	Low
Develop or apply concepts	High	High	Low	Low	Low
Take decisions	High	Medium	Medium	Low	Low
Explain techniques	Medium	Low	Low	High	Medium
Provide overview	Medium	Low	Low	High	Medium
Understand conflicting interests	Medium	Low	High	Low	Low
Initiate active communication	Medium	Medium	High	Low	Low
Motivate preparation for course	Low	High	Medium	Low	Low

A matrix allows a quick visual overview of performances evaluated against a set of criteria

- Limit the evaluation to three levels e.g. *high-medium-low* or *always-sometimes-never*. Beyond three rating levels, the differences are difficult to distinguish visually.

- Represent the ratings graphically e.g. black-grey-white, or by using decreasing dot sizes. Do not show ratings with numbers.

- Arrange the sequence of the criteria from best to worst performance so that a concentration of darker shading or big dots appears in the upper left corner of the matrix.
  This way, anomalies become more apparent.

POSITIONING maps show strategic positions and movements

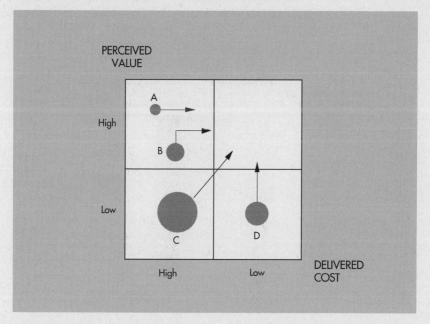

Positioning maps or grids help understand how products, competitors, activities, etc are positioned or moving in relation to each other along two dimensions.

- The two axes begin at the bottom left corner of the grid. If appropriate, the bottom left represents the worst performers while the top right represents the best.

- Vary the size of the bubble to represent a third dimension e.g. size of segment/brand.

- Place names next to the bubbles, add arrows to indicate movements and if appropriate, name areas to indicate distinct strategies.

A MAP combines geographical positions with data and flows

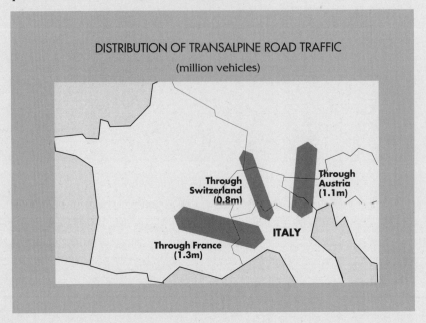

DISTRIBUTION OF TRANSALPINE ROAD TRAFFIC

(million vehicles)

Through Switzerland (0.8m)

Through Austria (1.1m)

Through France (1.3m)

ITALY

A map provides a geographical reference to information relating to positions, distances, flows, volume and densities.

- Sketch the boundaries according to the level of precision needed. Do not insert unnecessary details such as cities.
- Vary the thickness of flows in proportion to their volume.
- Use shading to stress relevant areas.

Maps are also a powerful way to highlight geographical share of a variable e.g. worldwide energy consumption. The size of regions or countries are distorted in relation to the relative share of their consumption.

For your notes:

ABOUT BCD

BCD are a group of trainers and management consultants who specialise in coaching managers communicate successfully within and outside their organisations. Examples of the added value BCD bring include:

- *Training managers to communicate effectively*

  Each year, BCD train nearly 1,000 managers and business school students from over 25 countries.

- *Assist managers to prepare their presentations*

  BCD help the presenter to extract, formulate and structure their messages. In addition, BCD can take over the creation and production of professional quality presentation materials.

- *Improving the content and delivery of training programmes*

  BCD offer their combined expertise in training and communication to help other trainers present their courses more effectively. This may involve conceiving the training structure, and creating visual supports and manuals.

BCD's clients come from a diverse and international base. They include organisations like ABB, Borden, CarnaudMetalbox, Club Med, Caterpillar, Center Parcs, Crédit Suisse, Du Pont, Hewlett-Packard, Logitech, Ernst & Young, Nestlé, Nokia Consumer Electronics, Piaget, Praxair, Ralston Energy Systems, Renault, Roche Consumer Health, SCA, Silicon Graphics, SNCF, Union Carbide, and the UN.
BCD also work closely with the IMD and HEC business schools in Lausanne, and the Center of Technology and Management (Zurich).

For more details of BCD's services, contact:

BCD Business Communication Design SA
80 av. C. F. Ramuz
CH-1009 Pully-Lausanne
Switzerland
Tel: (..41.21) 729 63 61 Fax: 729 70 30 e-mail: bcd@worldcom.ch